✓F29376

D0318844

CONTENTS

Readers are advised that there are images of Aboriginal people
now deceased contained in this book and that viewing those
images could cause distress in some Indigenous communities.

ABORIGINAL AUSTRALIANS
FIRST NATIONS OF AN ANCIENT CONTINENT

Stephen Muecke and Adam Shoemaker

Thames & Hudson

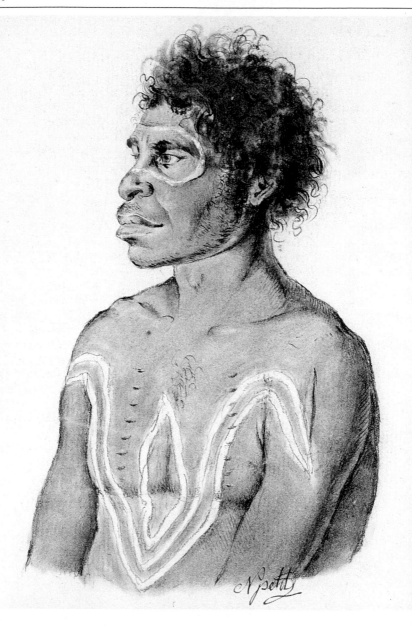

In the 18th century, as European colonization proceeded apace, one continent remained to be discovered, the mythical *Terra Australis Incognita*. This, the largest island-continent, had been inhabited for nearly sixty thousand years by the Aborigines, who were described by the first explorers as 'wandering bands of savages still living in the Stone Age'. This perception was the beginning of a deep and long-lasting cultural misapprehension.

CHAPTER 1

THE LAST CONTINENT

The 'Great Southern Land' has seen the longest continual occupation by an ancient culture anywhere in the world. This civilization did not present itself in ways that were easy for the Europeans to recognize: no monumental architecture, no cities. But the boomerang (left) clearly impressed the new arrivals, as Aborigines made it return accurately and demonstrated their hunting skills. Opposite, Aboriginal portrait by Nicolas Petit.

Looking for the Great Southern Land

It was often by accident that the first European ships landed in Australia. The strong westerlies coming across the Indian Ocean would tend to blow ships plying the East India trading route on to the Western Australian coast. So, in 1606, when the Dutch navigator Willem Jansz of the Dutch East India Company was gazing at the western side of Cape York Peninsula from the bridge of the *Duyfken*, he was sure that he had discovered the last continent, the 'Great South Land', whose existence had long been imagined by Europeans. The year 1616 saw Dirk Hartog's ship stranded on the Western Australian coast, where he left an inscribed pewter plate, the first material evidence of European contact with the new continent.

The explorers of the 15th and 16th centuries were in thrall to the mysterious southern continent. In 1547, Nicholas Yallard published an imaginary map, *Terra Australis Incognita* (above), which made it look like a rich, exotic and peaceful country.

Ever since the 16th century, the Portuguese, Dutch, Spanish and English had been engaging in lively trade in the Indian Ocean, and were on the lookout for the kind of rich lands mythologized by the likes of Marco Polo. So, when the Dutch first reached the island continent it was with a view to developing their trading advantage, but all they found was 'nothing profitable, only poor naked people walking along the beaches; without rice or many fruits'.

They were not immediately discouraged and for the next thirty years continued to explore the western, northern and southern coasts of this land that they had simply dubbed New Holland. The lack of the kind of natural resources they were looking for and the apparent poverty of the locals eventually made them decide

to extend their search for the Great Southern Land further to the east.

The English enter the picture

In 1688 William Dampier dropped anchor along the west Australian coast, making him the first Englishman to set foot on the continent. Looking for drinking water, he sent ten men armed with muskets and cutlasses, who captured two local men. This was his first contact with the Indigenous Australians, whom he described as the 'Miserablest People in the World', thus starting a trend to place them on the lowest rung of the scale of humanity.

The English captain James Cook was given a royal commission for the scientific and cartographic investigation of the Pacific and set sail for Tahiti in order to observe the passage of Venus between the Earth and the Sun. Cook was also charged to continue the search for the Great Southern Land, and having reached New Zealand, which he mapped, he pushed on to the east and eventually disembarked in a small bay on the eastern coast of Australia.

In 1642 Abel Tasman was ordered by the East India Company to explore the Gulf of Carpentaria in Australia's north. Reaching Australia via the south, he stopped on the south-west coast of the island known today as Tasmania, but which he named 'Van Diemen's Land' (above, a view of Schouten Island; opposite below, portrait of a young Bruny Island man, whose hair is decorated with red ochre). Tasman was disappointed because he found no valuable spices or fruits in the arid soil. His report to the Dutch did not enthuse them, so they abandoned their explorations in this part of the Pacific.

He called it Botany Bay because of the huge variety of plant life discovered there by the botanists in the expedition. Afterwards he headed north, charting as he went the eastern coast of the continent, and, failing to follow orders and gain 'the Consent of the Natives', took possession of the east coast of Australia in the name of King George III on 21 August 1770.

Cook keeps an open mind

The courage of the Aborigines impressed Cook from the moment he attempted to land on Botany Bay, 'As soon as we approached the rocks two of the men came down, each armed with a lance about ten feet long, and a short stick...resolved to dispute our landing to their utmost, though they were but two, and we were thirty or forty at least.' In his journal he later noted: 'they may appear to some to be the most wretched people on earth, but in reality they are far more happier than we Europeans' and adds '...unacquainted not only with the

A DESCRIPTION *of a wonderful large* WILD MAN, *or monstrous* GIANT, BROUGHT FROM BOTANY - BAY.

superfluous but the necessary Conveniences so much sought after in Europe, they are happy in not knowing the use of them...they seem'd to set no value upon any thing we gave them, nor would they ever part with anything of their own for any one article we could offer them.' What were the new colonists to do with these people with whom they shared no values? They could not trade with them for furs, spices, gold or ivory as in many other colonies. Apart from knives and steel axes, the Aborigines had no use for what the settlers had to offer.

The rather positive opinion that Cook brought to his encounter with the Indigenous Australians was not shared by most of the others who came there at that time or even later. For instance, the Spanish captain Alejandro Malaspina arrived in Sydney Cove on 12 March 1793 with José de Bustamente y Guerra and stayed a month in Port Jackson recording the

The European imagination fantasized the appearance of Aborigines, with a sailor from an English ship creating this giant, supposedly after seeing a Botany Bay native in 1789.

Sir Joseph Banks (1743–1820) was a wealthy naturalist who secured a place on Cook's 1770 voyage to Botany Bay in the *Endeavour*, which went as far as the Torres Strait. An avid Linnaean, he found much to interest him in Botany Bay, including the Banksia (below), which is named after him. Left, the first encounter with Aborigines in Port Jackson in 1788.

conditions and activities of the new colony. In extracts from his journal, he described at length the Aborigines as 'this wandering Nation, without agriculture and industry'.

French exploration in the 18th century

The French, as part of their scientific endeavour to broaden their knowledge of the natural sciences, were also exploring the Pacific seas. Marion du Fresne sailed into what is now Marion Bay, Tasmania, in 1772. Du Fresne came to the country expecting to find it inhabited with people similar to the 'noble savages' celebrated by Rousseau and other French explorers.

With this in mind he had two of his crew members strip naked and go ashore offering trinkets. The Aborigines showed little interest in what they had been offered but presented du Fresne with a burning brand. It is unclear what went wrong but stones and sticks were thrown and du Fresne and another officer were injured. Du Fresne went back to the longboats and attempted to land further along the beach only to be again threatened by the Aborigines. Du Fresne ordered his men to fire, resulting in the wounding and death of several Aborigines.

The next French vessel, captained by Jean-François de Galaup de La Pérouse, arrived in Australia in January 1788, a few days after the First Fleet had arrived at Botany Bay. La Pérouse was following orders to observe what the British were doing in New South Wales, and to study the possibility of colonial expansion in the region. He left after six weeks and was never seen again; his ships were later found wrecked off reefs near Vanuatu. The Revolution and Napoleon's Egyptian expedition brought a temporary halt to French interest in this part of the globe.

When the dust had settled on the domestic political scene, the French once again began to visit the Pacific and in 1800 sent Nicolas Baudin with the view to charting in detail some of the southern coast line, to collect specimens for the recently established Museum of Natural History, and to make anthropological observations – quite a new activity at the time – of the local Indigenous peoples. Before he left, the Society for the Observation of Man equipped him with *A Consideration of the Different Methods to be Followed in the Observation of Savage Peoples* by Joseph Marie de Gérando, the father of French anthropology.

In January 1802, he sailed from Sydney to the Bass Strait Islands and explored the western and southern coasts of Australia, collecting a vast number of specimens. But the most enduring aspects of his trip to Australia are the portraits done of the Tasmanian Aborigines in their natural habitat by two young artists in his expedition, Nicolas Petit and Charles-Alexandre Lesueur.

A first continent

The last continent to be discovered by the Europeans was also a first continent for the Aboriginal peoples.

At the end of their four-year expedition, Baudin's two ships, the *Géographe* and the *Naturaliste*, took away more than a hundred thousand specimens of animals: mammals, birds, reptiles, fish, molluscs and insects, including two and a half thousand unknown species. They also took on board living animals: emus, black swans and grey kangaroos (bottom). The discovery of the platypus (centre) and the echidna posed a real problem for the scientists: these animals were furry, suckled their young like mammals, but also sported a duck-bill (in the case of the platypus), a cloaca, and laid eggs! They had to create a new classification for these oviparous animals: monotremes. François Péron, the natural scientist on the Baudin expedition, reported his voyage in his *A Voyage of Discovery to the Southern Hemisphere* (1807). Despite its significant role in the history of science, this expedition did not have history on its side. Its legacy remains the superb watercolours by Petit and Lesueur (right), two artists who replaced the official draughtsmen, who disembarked because of illness.

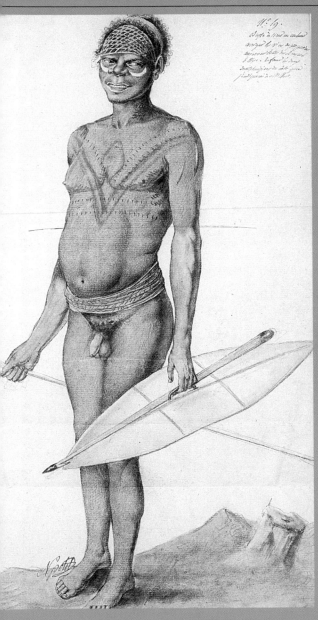

According to Péron, Nicolas Petit's drawings were a perfect record, even more valuable for the reason that they documented the Aborigines before colonization. Opposite above, Van Diemen's Land Aborigines carrying fire in their canoe; below, a family in front of their wind-break constructed out of linked pieces of bark. One man is posed in the traditional manner with one leg braced on the other. Left, a New Holland warrior with his wooden spear and shield.

•New Holland seems to be inhabited by a second race of men…different from those in Van Diemen's Land. They differ most from the latter by the lighter colour of their skin, by their long and smoother hair…. The cultivation of land and the use of metals are completely unknown to them, and, like the men of Van Diemen's Land, are without clothes, without any proper arts, without laws, or any clear ceremonies, no guaranteed mode of subsistence, so they are both obliged to go looking for nourishment in the middle of the forests or on the seashore.•
François Péron

Their occupation has been pushed back so far in time – up to 60,000 years – that it exceeds our capacity to measure it precisely.

In south-western New South Wales, not far from the Darling River, there are a series of former Pleistocene lake beds known as Lake Mungo. In the Pleistocene epoch, when these lakes contained water, people lived on the edges, fished and hunted near the lakes and occasionally buried their dead in the soft sand. In 1968, the cremated remains of a human skull were discovered and dated to about 25,000 years ago. Other sites of human occupation in the area have been dated to more than 40,000 years. This makes it the oldest human burial ground in Australia and possibly the earliest human cremation ground anywhere in the world.

It seems that after the ritual incineration the bones were smashed and placed in a hole by the pyre. This kind of practice – the ritual honouring of the dead – is a basic feature of human culture. Another burial site reveals that the body was covered in red ochre. Since there was no local source of ochre, it has been deduced that the material was carried there for ritual purposes. This is some of the earliest evidence for the deliberate choice of pigments in the South Pacific.

Another ochre discovery – the Nauwalabila Ochre Piece – was found in what is now Kakadu National Park in Australia's Northern Territory. The Nauwalabila fragment has been dated to in excess of 50,000 years, proving conclusively that Aboriginal occupation of Australia extends nearly 60,000 years into the past.

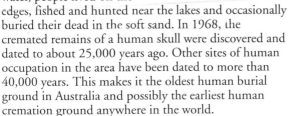

The limestone plateaux that dominate the plains in western Arnhem Land in the north of Australia conceal numerous caves decorated with paintings. The oldest still in existence date from as long as eighteen thousand years ago, and would have been created at the time of the last ice age when the level of the sea was a lot lower than it is now. The appearance of marine animals in the cave paintings seems to be concomitant with the rise of the sea level, at the end of this ice age, about ten thousand years ago. Above, a representation of the Crocodile Ancestor with a fish on the Obiri Rock (Kakadu National Park). Opposite, one of the sites at Lake Mungo.

How did the Aborigines come to be in Australia?

No one has a definitive answer. According to Indigenous Australian beliefs, the First Australians were 'born in the beginning' and have lived in the continent since time immemorial. Some archaeologists believe that successive waves of Aboriginal peoples colonized Australia from the north; others maintain that a founding population moved into northern Australia from South-East Asia 45,000 years ago and spread rapidly across all environments. There is considerable debate over the fact, nature and timescale of this movement.

If the first Australians did arrive from the north, they must have crossed an open sea, thousands of years before there is any evidence of anyone else in the world doing so. They went on to occupy the whole continent, developing strategies to accommodate every extreme of the landscape, from the driest deserts to snow-covered mountains and tropical rainforests. No people on earth have lived successfully for so long in such a diverse range of environments; it is generally accepted that the Aboriginal peoples can claim to have the oldest continuously maintained cultures on earth. But continuity does not mean that there was no change: prehistorians are still discovering many shifts in ideas and economy within a common framework.

Pre-colonial contacts

The Australian continent and its original inhabitants were never entirely isolated. Lower sea levels allowed direct contact by land with New Guinea and, even after the flooding of the north coast and the creation of Torres Strait about 6,000 years ago, there was much trade and contact between people on Cape York Peninsula and their northern neighbours.

In the early 18th century, the booming Chinese economy attracted primary products from the Indonesian archipelago. The most valuable commodity was trepang or dried sea cucumbers. Seafarers, especially those based in the port of Macassar, began to harvest and process the rich supplies of trepang around the north

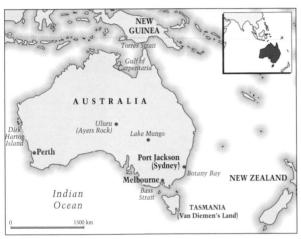

coast of Australia, particularly in Arnhem Land and, to a lesser degree, the Kimberley coast. Between about 1720 and the early 20th century, Aborigines in these areas had regular, seasonal contact with these visitors.

The Port Jackson penal colony

Compared to the arrival of the English in 1788, the annual fishing expeditions of the Macassans and Indonesians scarcely touched the Indigenous Australians. In 1787, Britain decided to create a penal colony in Australia to cater for the overflow from English prisons and, to some extent, those cast aside from the upheavals of the Industrial Revolution. The first vessels set sail from Portsmouth in May of that year.

In this painting at Nourlangie Rock in Kakadu (opposite, above left), Namarrgon can be seen on the left. He is the Lightning Spirit, with bolts of lightning (on the right) and his wife on the left. This style of painting, which lets us see the internal organs and the spine of the figures, is known as 'X-Ray' painting. It goes back some 7,000 years and is still practised in Arnhem Land on rocks, bark, or even canvas.

Indigenous knowledge is transmitted orally, so epic texts are learned by ritual repetition. A senior singer can thus, like Homer, sing a song narrative continuously over many hours without error. It is often assumed that this orality makes Aboriginal cultures pre-literate ones, but in fact, while language was not inscribed phonetically (with a symbol for each sound), meanings were inscribed on various materials, including the body, with an abstract iconography of lines, concentric circles, dots. Such iconography would also be employed as sand drawing while telling a story, and on sacred boards and stones called *tjurunga* in the central desert (opposite below, rock art). This rich iconography now provides the basis for much contemporary art.

The next year, the First Fleet of British colonists arrived in eleven ships. Led by Captain Arthur Phillip, they reached Sydney Cove, a little to the north of Botany Bay, on 26 January, and started clearing trees, building and growing crops. There were 290 seamen, soldiers and officers and 717 convicts, nearly as many as the local Aboriginal people, the Gamaraigal. The locals observed the construction of the first Australian town, on the site of the

present city of Sydney. For the first year they kept their distance, apart from the occasional tentative contact. Relations became closer after the first of a series of smallpox epidemics that struck Port Jackson in April 1789. The effect of these was not just a massive loss of numbers: within the tightly knit kinship system, the loss of this proportion of people also meant that whole swathes of knowledge and the capacity to carry out ceremonies would be difficult to recover.

Most of the new arrivals were English and Irish convicts convicted for minor infringements, due mainly to their impoverished circumstances in the old country. The first years were very hard to endure as food and clothing were in short supply. The convicts and soldiers led a rough life where rum was a currency of exchange, and they tended to be contemptuous of the 'savages', whom they could treat as a lower order than themselves. Drawn into this alcoholic culture, the Aborigines could sometimes be seen fighting in the streets amongst each other, an 'entertainment' urged on by onlookers. Only the officer class permitted themselves more human or scientific observations, like Watkin Tench, who noted that the pleasing softness and timidity of the Aboriginal women was evidence of normal human sensibilities. When a convict who had stolen fishing tackle from the natives was flogged in front of them to demonstrate civilized notions of justice, he noted

that the 'savages' were revolted and the women moved to tears.

Bennelong

The first Governor of New South Wales, Arthur Phillip was impatient to make contact with the Aborigines. In November 1789, he captured Bennelong and Colbee, who were both survivors of the early smallpox epidemic. Phillip's intention was to 'open intercourse with the natives, and to conciliate their affections'. There was also the expectation that the new settlers would 'live in

Eighteen years after James Cook's voyage, Arthur Phillip chose Sydney Cove as the site for the establishment of the first penal colony (below). Opposite above, English convicts about to leave for Botany Bay from the port of Plymouth, 1792.

amity and kindness with them'. Bennelong and Phillip formed a close relationship. Phillip even took him to be presented King George III, as evidence of successful diplomacy in the new penal colony. Watkin Tench found him impressive: 'His powers of mind were certainly far beyond mediocrity. He acquired the knowledge both of our manners and language, faster than his predecessor had done. He willingly communicated information; sang, danced and capered: told us all the customs of his country, and all the details of his family economy. Love and war seemed his favourite pursuits; in both of which he had suffered severely.'

In 1790, at Bennelong's request, a brick hut was built for him on the east point of Sydney Cove on the land now known as Bennelong Point (the site of the Sydney Opera House). Bennelong scarcely used the hut, although it became a meeting place for Aboriginal people. This was their dancing ground; their stamping feet raised dust in the light of fires as they performed the first corroborees viewed by the Europeans. Bennelong's associations with the whites made it hard for him to survive in his own community. Why would they trust him now that he was consorting with the 'ghosts'? With rum being a currency, Bennelong himself succumbed to drink and procured it for his own people, to the dismay of the tribal elders.

A clash of cultures

From their point of view, it seems Aborigines were both repulsed by, and attracted to, the white settlements and what was going on there. Bennelong – who was known as a master of mimicry – was just one of many Indigenous Australians who concentrated their attention upon

what they saw as the strange, illogical habits of the European invaders. Faced with an abundance of fresh fish in the waterways of the colony, the Governor of New South Wales and his entourage turned up their noses at this bounty, preferring six-month-old salted cod from England. The English settlers initially went hungry rather than eat kangaroo, and while they had to admire the uncanny Aboriginal tracking skills and the skilled use of boomerang and spear, their own idea of hunting was the importation of English foxes and the strange ritual of hunting an animal they had no intention of eating. For the Aborigines such behaviour was an endless source of amusement. They were also horrified at the whites' treatment of each other and their rape of the environment, cutting and slashing in order to build and plant. They clashed with whites over resources and when their sacred places were disrespected.

But at the same time they were keen to acquire objects like steel axes and tobacco. Along with flour, tea and sugar, these commodities had far-reaching effects and were destined to have a huge impact on the local economy and social structure. Stone axes used to be in the exclusive possession of powerful older Aboriginal men, so when a steel axe was obtained by a woman or younger man, this superior artefact would destabilize the internal power dynamics of the community. And while there was a native tobacco in existence, *pituri*, Aborigines would travel miles to seek out the introduced tobacco. Edward

Bungaree (opposite) liked to dress up as an English officer. He accompanied Matthew Flinders on his 1802–3 circumnavigation of Australia, a major mapping achievement. Bennelong was the first Australian Aborigine to have sustained relations with Europeans, and was even taken to England in 1793. He was presented to King George III by the first governor of New South Wales, Arthur Phillip, along with kangaroos, dingoes and bright parrots, in order to demonstrate his successful assimilation into the new penal colony. Above, soldiers at Botany Bay, in around 1790.

Curr, writing in 1840s recalls that 'the words, terrible from their repetition, *i inyanook bakka, mitta cowel, ingarnika!* (give little tobacco, Mr Curr smallest) rang forever in my ear.' Aborigines were aware of the destructive effects of alcohol, and some tried to avoid it. Others found themselves drawn into its economy. Like other commodities, it was used for exchange on the frontier where the exploitation of Aboriginal women's sexuality also became part of an integrating economy where most white men were both drinkers and bachelors.

From misunderstanding to inevitable confrontation

The Aborigines' response to the invaders was varied: in some cases armed resistance; in others accommodation or adaptation; in many instances they moved further away from the invaders, whom they perhaps did not expect to last long in Australia anyway. In some Aboriginal languages, the name given to the European invaders was the same as for spirits of the dead, or of corpses, for Aborigines knew that the corpses of their

The daily life of Aborigines (above, illustration by Nicolas Petit, early 19th century) took place in camps of about fifty people who were related by the kinship system. Women and men left in the early morning on separate hunting and foraging parties, coming back in time to share the spoils according to set rules, cooking and resting in the heat of the day. Children learnt by watching, listening and imitating their parents and were discouraged from asking too many questions. Adults also discussed cultural life while making useful, decorative or sacred artefacts from the available materials.

own dead lost their pigmentation and went white. But once they understood that these white people were invaders, who had the intention of settling permanently on their ancestral lands and taking the best land, a logic of resistance began. The friendly curiosity of the first encounters gave way to confrontation.

What were the new colonists to do with these people with whom they shared no values? They could not trade with them for furs, spices, gold or ivory as in many other colonies. They could not understand an attachment to country that was not based on agricultural 'improvement'. Because the first Europeans could discern no ostensible government or clear leadership structure among the locals, there was no discussion of a treaty. So, at the end of this first chapter in Australia's history, the political settlement between the existing inhabitants and the invading colonists was unresolved, and it remains so to this day.

Decimated by disease, the Eora and Gadigal peoples of the Sydney region mingled with new arrivals, people from inland and other coastal regions. They were drawn to the city (above, a print from 1830) because of their dislocation from their homelands and consequent poverty. They would often camp in the boatsheds at Circular Quay, making demands for boats and land, demands that were amplified by their drinking in public. By 1882 the government of the colony appointed a Protector of Aborigines to investigate the situation and make recommendations.

The ceremonies of the Indigenous Australians make life rise up from the land, travel along it, and go down into the soil again. Their philosophy emphasizes the spiritual over the material, though the spiritual is not transcendent; it exists in the here and now, in parallel with our everyday human lives, and in modest, respectful and intimate contact with all other things. Laws governing human relationships link some five hundred tribal groups as they follow the flux of abundance across the whole continent.

CHAPTER 2
A CULTURE CELEBRATING LIFE

In the beginning, say many Dreamings, the earth was a vast unformed plain. Then ancestor beings began to stir and break the surface, transforming themselves into landforms, animals, plants, and all things of the world. These Dreaming ancestors (bark painting, right) began epic journeys above or below the country, leaving their marks, naming all the places, singing life into things and leaving a massive culture whose signs were there to be read: constellations in the sky, powerful rivers, sacred places. Opposite, an Indigenous man from the central desert region.

Hunters and gatherers

Traditionally gatherers and hunters, Indigenous
Australians have developed a sustainable relationship
with their countries over many generations. They did
not enclose domestic animals nor accumulate goods to
any great extent; they combined their hunting skills with
knowledge of animal behaviour and ecology. Australia is
blessed with a hugely diverse biosphere, so Indigenous
Australians have an extensive menu: from turtles and
shellfish to honey ants, grubs, moths, lizards, berries
and grass seeds. Women, specializing in vegetable foods,
know the locations of yam patches and will not exhaust
them. Gathering vegetable foods is a staple activity,
less subject to chance that the hunt for large animals,
especially in the arid and semi-arid desert regions, where
water is also found and conserved with expert skill.

Living in Aboriginal country usually meant travelling
on a seasonal basis from one place to another within a

Depending on the
place and time,
hunting and gathering
provided a plentiful diet
and left ample time for
cultural pursuits, which
in turn added meaning
to the basic activities of
life (above, taking bark
from a mangrove tree
to make a shield). Such
a life seems satisfying
and simple, but there
are no guarantees. In
some seasons people
enjoy an abundance,
but at another time
food and water can
be in short supply.

fairly circumscribed home country, governed usually by the availability of food, but also by the cultural requirement to attend ceremonies. Only essential tools would be carried from place to place. Women usually have a digging stick for searching for yams and killing small animals, a basket, and perhaps a wooden coolamon, used as a cradle or for winnowing seeds. Grass seeds are ground on stones left at camping site, and made into bread.

For hunting, men use spears whose range and speed they can double with the leverage of a woomera, a spear-thrower. They also use boomerangs in open territory to knock down birds, or indeed they might use traps of various sorts. The appearance of a certain migratory bird on the coast is a sign that the fish are running. According to Aboriginal knowledge, they are then ready to be caught in large numbers using traditional fishing nets or traps made of stone walls, which imprison the fish as the tide runs out.

An economical management of natural resources

The first Europeans to visit Aboriginal communities could see no signs of agriculture or 'tilling the soil' as they understood it. But Aboriginal people did farm in an ecologically sensitive fashion. For example, the killing of too many of one species – or of juvenile animals – was prohibited. Certain categories of people (for instance women or uninitiated men) were not permitted to eat particular foodstuffs.

Another technique of collecting food was firestick farming, carried out only at the end of the dry season. The intentional burning of grass and low scrub would flush out animals. It would also create the essential conditions for the regeneration of certain native Australian plants and animals, which normally depended on lightning strikes to cause the bush

The kangaroo is a prized animal for hunters, as depicted in the bark painting below, which depicts a *mimi* spirit spearing the creature.

fires that would enable their propagation. In the middle of the 19th century the German explorer Ludwig Leichhardt noted that the people 'seemed to have burned the grass systematically along every watercourse, and around every waterhole, in order to have them surrounded with young grass as soon as the rain sets in….' The Aborigines would thus have open ground to stalk the animals that would come to graze there. Finally, this was an aesthetic issue, and the country would become easier to walk through. All of this encapsulates the balanced nature of life and of Indigenous Australian attitudes towards living. Theirs was an environment that was more like a provident parent than a source of produce, more a religious shrine than a physical space. So economic and ecological activities are accompanied by ritual work. There is a Honey Ant Dreaming (a set of songs, an iconography, and a ceremony), which is performed to remind people of the importance of the honey ant in their cosmos, to express their custodial relationship and to ensure the increase of the honey ant.

The Dreaming

Indigenous Australian society centres around the concept of the Dreaming. This term has nothing to do with a somnolent or 'dreamlike' approach to the external world

Women, from an early age, learn to make baskets and mats from natural fibres (far right). Firestick farming (above) continues to the present day.

Different types of housing include beehive-shaped clay huts, shelters made with branches and leaves (opposite below) and in the north, slabs of bark.

or to the inner self. Instead it refers to an embracing ideology – and accompanying spiritual belief – about the creation of the universe as well as a relationship of balance and harmony with all things in it. The Dreaming therefore implies a code of conduct, a form of behaviour, and a pattern of life. It implies active custodianship (of land, of sacred sites, of relationships with people), as well as acceptance of doctrinal rules.

Significantly, the Dreaming, despite the fact that sometimes it is rendered in English as 'the Dreamtime', is atemporal. It is not a chronological concept (like the biblical Genesis) but a focus on, and a vital connection with, ancestral beings who travelled the length and breadth of the continent, forming the natural features of the landscape and social relationships with humankind at the same time. Those beings go by many regionally specific names – the Rainbow Serpent, the Wandjina, the Lightning Brothers – and they exist today as they always have and always will. Thus, the Dreaming is 'always already' and it is both epistemology

In many regions, the hot climate and absence of modesty allowed people not to wear any clothes, or perhaps just a pubic cover hanging from a hair-string belt, which also held an axe. But in the cold southern regions cloaks were made from kangaroo or possum skin. Women would cut their hair and spin it to make belts for their loved ones, and they would wear hair ornaments made from a spray of multicoloured parrot feathers attached to a wooden pin.

These photographs are the memories of a time now past, for Port Macquarie, where they were taken in 1905, is now a booming tourist resort. The local people are known as Birpai, as they were then, but much of their world has changed. Memory is an essential part of the maintenance of culture. Only in the last twenty years have the history books started to recognize that there was an important history preceding white settlement. This history has emerged from under the official record, as the tools of memory – photographs, oral histories and archival documents – have released information and found contexts for its use. Local and family histories are popular, and in museums there is now always an Indigenous presence. Tourists from all over the world enjoy the beaches and sport fishing at this seaside town, and they are also fascinated by Indigenous history. Local Indigenous leaders can demonstrate the power of memory as they tell the tourists that there was a time when the coastline was a different shape, or that there were active volcanoes in the area. Such memories, going back 10,000 years or more, have been confirmed by scientists.

and ontology; a way of knowing and a way of being. Anthropologist W. E. H. Stanner expressed the atemporal nature of Aboriginal philosophy by characterizing the Dreaming as 'everywhen', capturing its spatial and temporal ubiquity.

'My father is that tree'

According to Indigenous Australian beliefs, the creation beings gave order to a formless world: great snakes churned the country creating rivers, laying eggs that were mountains. Life was thus spawned, spread and differentiated in all the places of the world. The creators were, and still are, spirits, human beings, ancestors, and concrete things. They are all these at once: for example, for the Nyigina, a certain mountain is a woman in repose, who is *nalyag* (the blue-tongue lizard), who is also all the people who belong to that lizard clan. The many-levelled simultaneity of these beliefs is one of their most important distinguishing features.

The creation stories – just like the ceremonial songs that are chanted as one travels the country, encountering sacred sites – keep this multiple sense of being in flux. People can be sure about their belonging *in places*; historical time becomes far less important. The power that created the world resides in these physical locations. When an Aboriginal man or woman travels to one of these sacred places they put their bodies in the locus of creation and of continuity. Thus, the power that resides there not only recognizes them but also inspires them to act.

When Aboriginal people speak of legends and stories, they invoke a mythology that is

Bark paintings reflect the rich spiritual life of the artists and draw on sacred themes and ritual designs. Some images are more restricted than others and some may never be produced for a wider public. Above, Namarrgon, Thunder Spirit; opposite right, the Rainbow Serpent.

Wandjina (left) are mythological figures from the northern Kimberley region. Magnificent paintings of these ancestral spirits adorn many caves in the deep and inaccessible bush. As the seasons change with the approach of the monsoon rains, the increased humidity causes the colours in the cave paintings to 'come alive' as the hues deepen, a practical and symbolic example of reanimation.

sacred because it is always there: it resides in locations, places that must be approached with reverence. The spirits of babies come from similar places, and other locations will confer upon individuals a clan or totemic identity that is not separate from or representing them, but is *at one* with them.

The key to spiritual health in traditional Aboriginal society is, therefore, a constant renewal of the relationship with Dreaming ancestors. It is possible for individuals to have meaningful connections with several Dreamings; some are relatively static while others travel huge distances and animate entire regions of the Australian continent. The reiteration of stories, the creation and re-creation of song and dance, the expression of art, all partake of the continual renaissance of connection between human beings and the Dreaming.

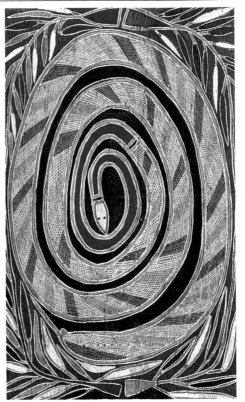

Reading the country

The country contains traces of the Dreaming events that took place there. Stories speak of the Eternal Ancestors and their creation of the characteristics of the places (a tree, a rock, a spring of fresh water). So space is not merely a geographical extension, but carries a particular significance for religion and identity. For example, one notices a spot where an ancestor collected bush onion, and therefore stops to harvest it again, or remembers that in a specific waterhole lies the danger of a malevolent spirit, and therefore passes it by. The shape and meaning of the landscape is thus the Aboriginal heritage.

Yurlunggul, the Rainbow Serpent, is a major mythological figure in northern Australia. It deposits conception spirits in waterholes and is responsible for bringing rains, but if someone disturbs it or breaks the law, it can send floods and thunderstorms. It can also swallow people and regurgitate their bones, which turn into stone, thus remaining as a document of the story.

Each Indigenous person, as the embodiment of an Ancestral life-force, has spiritual links with specific sites in the country. This link is inalienable and cannot be transferred to another place. As custodian of the Dreaming, he or she is also custodian of the associated places and itineraries; these are celebrated with rituals during which the myths are told, painted, danced and sung.

But these ritual tracks sometimes cover many hundreds of kilometres, so the rituals, the sets of mythic knowledge, and responsibilities for custodianship are spread across the countries of different tribal groupings. A mythic narrative, which is often a 'song cycle', can stretch across half the continent and is therefore shared and cut up by different communities with distinct languages. Only when they gather as a group can the totality of the mythic cycle be reproduced. Here 'managers' (known as *kurdungurlu* in the central desert) make sure the 'owners' (*kirda*) get the words and the

Uluru (above) in central Australia is one of the most sacred Indigenous sites. In 1985 it was handed back to the Yankunytjatjara and Pitjantjatjara peoples, who now lease it as a national park. Nearly every feature of the rock has meaning; there are springs and cave paintings marking the passage of Mala (wallaby) and the snakes Kuniya (python) and Liru (poisonous snake). In the story the Liru were boys who threw spears at Kuniya and killed him. He was avenged by his aunt who killed one of the Liru.

Each mythological story is associated with a territory under the custodianship of several families. It is their responsibility to re-enact the sacred history of their ancestors and in the process pass the information about their travels on to future generations. They do this with the help of iconic representations, traditionally done with body paint, on bark, as ground paintings or as rock art. Most recently they have been transposed to canvas, and the key icons remain: concentric circles, parallel lines or arcs. These motifs seem abstract to the uninitiated, but for the knowledgeable there are complex intersections of meaning and power. For them the painting does not represent something absent, but creates the presence of its content. The patterns of the lines are designed to create a shimmering effect that is part of the aesthetic. This painting by Ronnie Tjampitjinpa of the Pintupi in central Australia (above left) represents the travels of the Tingari Ancestors.

sequencing right. At such a meeting ownership might be publicly passed on to someone younger, thus assuring the continuity of the tradition.

The intimate knowledge Indigenous Australians have of country, and the form this knowledge takes, is a product of living off the land and of the collaborative effort needed to reproduce and pass on cultural material. It produces an extremely strong feeling of belonging, which is, of course, not a proprietorial sense, for the land cannot be sold, fought for or given away. Its identity is shared among all things in it.

Travelling cultures

Traditional Aboriginal people travelled for many reasons within a defined geographical region. They travelled to find food in season, or they arranged to arrive in meeting places at a certain time of year to perform ceremonies, organize marriages, and to trade goods. On these trips men would carry their spears, woomeras and boomerangs (or more likely today, guns); the women carried the babies, digging sticks and baskets. Shelters would be built at each camp; people would sleep between small fires and in the company of their dogs. A group of people walking swiftly with a relaxed, energy-efficient gait could cover many kilometres in a day. Often it was very long way between waterholes. Different clans respected the country of their neighbours and did not normally trespass upon it – but they were usually connected to each other through kinship and shared ownership of mythological stories.

It is noteworthy that land is defined less by boundaries, and much more by the sacred places and the tracks that cross the land. These tracks are important both as the pathways of the ancestors, and as the trading routes that people still follow today. Indigenous Australian cultures are maintained through the act of singing the songs, and telling the stories of the places as one arrives at them. These are, therefore, cultures of travel. Moving across the land reinforces a sense of belonging to it.

Dreamings and rituals

A primary importance is given by Indigenous Australians to the rituals and ceremonies that affirm and strengthen the links they have with country and with the Dreaming spirits. As a receptacle for the collective memory, it is through ritual that knowledge is reinforced, memorized and passed on.

Sometimes death is seen as a traumatic event for which a responsible person must be found. Funerals are extremely important because a person's spirit cannot rejoin the creation spirits unless it is put to rest in an appropriate manner. These ceremonies differ greatly from one place to another. Some bury their dead in caves in the hills, some cremate them, others leave a wrapped body on a platform or wedged in a tree trunk. Funeral rites can last

Bush camps (above) are often at 'good places' designated in the ancient myths. Like the ancestors, people will move on, leaving the temporary structures behind.

It is much easier to hunt in a group (left) than alone, and grass fires can be used to flush out animals. These days it is easier to bring down bush turkeys with a gun rather than a boomerang, then the catch has to be carried back to camp, where it is shared among all the relatives according to their age and status. Kangaroo is cooked in a ground oven. First the fur is singed off on a large fire built in a sandy place, the legs are broken and the spleen removed. It is buried in the hot coals of the fire for about three hours, by which time it is nicely roasted. The eucalyptus wood with which it is cooked gives it a uniquely Australian flavour. It is cut up and distributed, and the liver and tail are delicacies. Other large animals like dugongs, turtles, goannas, crocodiles and emus are cooked in a similar way. The Indigenous Australian kitchen has a huge range of flavoursome meats, seafoods and vegetables.

several months and are almost always accompanied by prohibitions: silence on the part of widows, or wiping out the personal name from everyday usage. In the case of a common name like Bill, this might mean not using that word for an invoice, or calling another man called Bill by his kin name alone. Some members of the clan may have to change their names after a death.

Initiation rites are the other most important life ceremony, especially for men; the child symbolically dies to give birth to the man. In the first years of his or her life, the child is brought up by the extended family, including aunts and uncles and by the camp in general where tasks are shared around. Young children live without any responsibility and in relative freedom. As an adolescent, a boy slowly begins to leave the women's camp to join the men's expeditions and to begin his male apprenticeship, followed by the initiation at about fourteen. This crucial ritual is accompanied by periods of

isolation, food taboos and initiatory trips to visit sacred sites and to visit distant relatives. Finally the initiation ceremony is linked to a major Dreaming as the boy 'dies' only to be reborn and reintegrated with the community as a whole. At the turning point of the ceremony there is usually some kind of physical ordeal: scarification, circumcision, tooth avulsion. Females are excluded from these sacred rites, just as men are from those of women. The boys undergoing them are introduced to the secret meanings of stories they have been partly familiar with, key concepts are introduced, which they must keep secret, and they acquire a degree of knowledge that will be augmented throughout life.

Kinship: genius of Aboriginal peoples

In the 1960s Claude Lévi-Strauss described Aboriginal people as intellectual aristocrats. Anthropology thus speaks of Aborigines as modern people who had developed elaborate social systems for being together, assuring their

Preparing for the ceremony (above) can take hours, longer than the performance. But in this time people may tease and joke, as well as interpreting for the young boy the serious content of the myth as it is being inscribed on his body. In this way the Dreaming is made manifest in the present: the boy becomes his 'totem' once again. Instruction is thus associated with the pleasure of being treated as a special person by the older men. After the dance the boy's paints quickly wear off, but the lessons remain.

survival in a harsh environment. Kinship systems are like complex mathematics: much time is spent learning them, discussing them and carrying out the obligations and enjoying the privileges that flow from their rules. Many European children scarcely know who their aunts and uncles are, but Aboriginal children can reel off a whole series of kinship names and relationships from an early age. Indigenous societies are governed more on the basis of kinship rules, than on leadership or merit.

Kin are both biological and classificatory. This means that while there is a biological mother, all her sisters are also classified as 'mother' by her children. A child will address all these women quite happily as 'mummy'. In some parts of Australia, people belong to one of four or eight main groups and classes, which in part summarize their kinship relations to other members of their society. Specific relationships have rules. Mothers-in-law are avoided, a boy's maternal uncle has responsibility for educating him through the passages to adulthood, and the optimal marriage partner is often one kind of cousin.

Visitors to Aboriginal communities often find themselves integrated into the community after a short time by being given a kinship name, for instance 'brother', by someone who was their first point of contact. Once this is established – for instance in the terms used by the Nyigina people, one's 'skin' name is *jungarrayi*, henceforth all other *jungarrayi* are now 'brother' – then all others in the community will now know how to address you and what they can ask you to do. *Jungarrayi* might now find the odd *nangala*

The two Wawilak Sisters (left, depicted on a hollow-log coffin) are fertility gods of the Yolngu in Arnhem Land and are the daughters of Djanggawul, a major ancestor deity. In one story, the sisters pollute a sacred waterhole and anger the resident Great Python, who coils around them, swallows and disgorges them. This episode forms the basis of the initiation rites where the 'disgorging' of youths creates men. The act of swallowing and regurgitation also divides the tribe into moieties, two ritually distinct groups, the Dhuwa and Yirritja. Above, a bark painting of a funerary ritual.

('wife') looking fondly at him, or a young *japangardi* ('nephew') put in his charge. If he moves, even thousands of kilometres, to another community and can cite his skin name, then he is once again instantly integrated.

Religion, magic and ritual

'Ntjipurara, the leader of the combined hosts, sat down with his legs crossed under him. The *iliara* seated themselves around him in circles. They all opened their veins. Thereupon a wondrous river of blood swallowed them all; it engulfed them deep in the ground; the blood rose to the top. Underneath the surface of the ground they continued their journey....'

This account, from 1946, was told by a white man, T. G. H. Strehlow, the son of a missionary, who was brought up with the Arrernte of Central Australia and spoke their language perfectly. Such a story, of a subterranean river of blood used for travelling unseen through the country of unfriendly neighbours, is a powerful poetic image that is integrated into the ceremonial practices of the tribe: blood is frequently used in the ceremonies. Such a fantastic image speaks of the

The native tobacco or *pituri*, which contained nicotine, was extensively traded before colonization. It came mostly from an area in south-west Queensland where one group had a specialization, curing the plant by smoking the leaves and trading it over long distances. Rich ochres were carried from South Australia, and axe-heads came from the north. *Pituri* was mixed with acacia ashes and chewed. Once stronger tobacco arrived with the Europeans, it was generally preferred, and was a major factor in bringing tribespeople into missions. Above, women and children from the Tully River area, Queensland.

power of the great mysteries of life, and of the elders' mastery of these mysteries. To believe in the potency of such images is to assent, as all cultures do, to the possibility that there is more to the human spirit than simply the mundane and the practical.

In other parts of the country we might learn about *rai*, spirits, and how they create *maban* or shamans by giving them new insides; maban have an 'third eye' by which they will see what is normally invisible, and an 'aerial or astral rope' with which they will be able to travel through the air or under the ground. In yet another location, we learn of liquefied quartz being sung all over and into initiates' bodies, so they can grow feathers and fly. We hear of people being able to reduce their size to a few centimetres or grow to prodigious proportions. Stories of the ability to take out and replace one's internal organs abound. And if you linger by the seashore in the north-west you may be privileged to catch a glimpse of *ngadjayi*, sea-nymphs.

These are the powers of the men and women of great knowledge as described in A. P. Elkin's *Aboriginal Men of High Degree*. This knowledge, while exclusive and

One day an old *maban* or shaman in a camp north of Broome was watching a group of women leave camp. His special powers enabled him to see the *rai* (the spiritual origin of children) flitting around them as they walked. When they came back later in the day he looked again and called out: 'One *rai* missing!' All the women got excited then, and asked each other, giggling, 'Who among us is going to get this baby?' They knew that the Ancestors had disseminated a limited number of *rai*, and the *rai* had entered one of them. Above, an Aboriginal camp in Queensland, 1940s.

gradually acquired during one's lifetime, does not create priests as such, for there was no institution of religion in traditional life. There was a ceremonial way of life, shot through with powerfully poetic images and mysterious forces. The story this culture told about human life and death was not one of redemption, transcendence to a better place, or reincarnation, but it was a narrative that stressed assent to the laws of the ancestor beings spiritually embodied in places. The positive presence of ancestors (who are always also other beings and things) is made to emerge through vitalistic performances. Good things are brought into being, and evil tends to lie external to the community in the form of devils and malevolent spirits.

Anthropologist W. E. H. Stanner expressed both the beauty and power of Aboriginal philosophy: 'The whole religious corpus vibrated with an expressed aspiration for life, abundant life. Vitality, fertility and growth; the conservation, production, protection and rescue of life ...apparently animated phenomena such as green leaves, rain and the seasons, lightning, whirlwinds, shooting stars and the heavenly bodies; or things of unexplained origin, unusual appearance and giant size.'

So many Aboriginal stories seem to culminate in metamorphoses: beings turning into trees, stars or tracks. But these are not everyday stories, they are magical stories that are part and parcel of the strong

Incest, greed and violation of sacred laws are the major Aboriginal crimes. Agreement is reached among the elders (above) on the nature of the punishment and the guilty party nearly always submits in good grace. For minor offences, people are made to feel ashamed through public ridicule or abuse. They can be threatened with supernatural intervention, sorcery or banishment. A common punishment is spearing through the thigh, with onlookers who control the participants. Sorcery performed through magical songs, or the famous 'pointing the bone'.

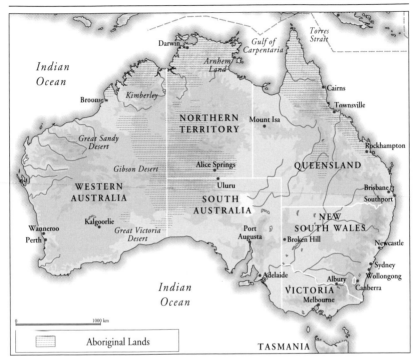

The map shows place names including:

Indian Ocean · Torres Strait · Darwin · Gulf of Carpentaria · Arnhem Land · Broome · Kimberley · Cairns · Townsville · NORTHERN TERRITORY · Mount Isa · Great Sandy Desert · Rockhampton · Gibson Desert · Alice Springs · QUEENSLAND · WESTERN AUSTRALIA · Uluru · SOUTH AUSTRALIA · Brisbane · Southport · NEW SOUTH WALES · Wanneroo · Kalgoorlie · Great Victoria Desert · Port Augusta · Broken Hill · Newcastle · Perth · Sydney · Wollongong · Adelaide · Albury · Canberra · Indian Ocean · VICTORIA · Melbourne · TASMANIA

0 ____ 1000 km

Aboriginal Lands

beliefs and rituals that intensify the bodily energies of the participants in the ceremony. A ritual performance is an event where codes (music, dance, myth, organization of space) that are normally quite separate in everyday life are brought together and condensed so that actual transformations can be brought about on the bodies of the participants, or a single participant: an initiate to be made into a man and imbued with knowledge, or a sick person to be cured. These bodies 'turn into' the body of the ancestor-snake, or the pain in the body is transformed into, for instance, a shard of quartz.

Law and knowledge

As in the traditional past, so today, knowledge and power are distributed in Aboriginal communities in a spirit of consent and according to a principle of custodianship.

The Indigenous Australians once occupied the whole continent, but the present communities mostly live in the central desert areas, the north (Arnhem Land or the Kimberley), the Western Desert, Queensland and the Torres Strait (above).

Sharpened stone for axes was fixed to handles with the tendon from a kangaroo tail and spinifex wax hardened after being heated. Spears and other tools (opposite below) were crafted with care.

Even if there are no Indigenous Australians living today as they did sixty thousand years ago, this does not mean that key elements of the traditional life have not persisted in tandem with modernity. Older people, with greater knowledge, wield the most power, but even that is limited by the rules of custodianship. It is customary to defer authority, by saying that one will have to go to another person for the continuation of that line of knowledge. Knowledge is not treated as personal property but is destined to be passed on to the younger generation, who then acquire the status of senior custodians.

In traditional Indigenous life, trade and economic exchange was regulated in a cultural fashion. Its gestures were both tied up with kinship obligations and were deeply symbolic. One example can be given from the Ngarrindjeri in South Australia. In the old days when a Ngarrindjeri child was born, its umbilical cord was dried and treated, bundled in feathers and sent in exchange to another group of people with a new-born child. The two children, thus linked, then had a special life-long relationship. Gifts of food and weapons accompanied the exchanges, but the main role of the partners was to act as intermediaries in trade relations between their respective groups.

Certain parts of the country were rich in resources not available elsewhere. Latterly, pearl shell from the north-west coast was traded right through central Australia, and the

In order to perform their clan rites, men from the Warlpiri and Waramunga groups in the desert inscribe their bodies with the local designs connected to the rite. Feathers and down or wild kapok are stuck on with blood; ochres and vegetable dyes colour the designs. Sometimes headdresses are made with bark and other materials, belts are woven with women's hair, and ritual objects are carried during the dances. These old photographs (left and opposite below) show a degree of preparation rarely seen today.

country of the Kalkatungu – renowned warriors – was rich in stones for axe-heads. Certain ochres were valuable for painting in rock shelters or on the body. All these things were traded, and sometimes foods, and very often people from different tribal groupings would gather together at a place and a time when fish could easily be trapped, or to harvest a certain kind of moth rich in fat. Here trade would take place, ceremonies would be performed, marriages arranged and love-affairs surreptitiously enjoyed.

Such meetings reinforced the cultural continuities between groups as, for instance, a whole ceremonial song cycle might be produced as an important cultural event; hours would be spent in enjoyable gossip as the dancers were painted with the 'signature' designs that signified the clan countries. Feathers might be stuck on to the body with congealed blood donated from the arm of a man, or elaborate headdresses constructed out of human hair, clay and spinifex wax. Others would organize the singing groups. Here custodians of the different parts of the song, celebrating perhaps the deeds of ancestor-beings travelling the countryside, would make sure that the different parts that each person 'owned' would link together correctly. Only through such meetings could the song cycle be fully and correctly performed. In this way, these people from different groups, with their ancient advisors and little children participating, came together to celebrate their culture and to celebrate life.

Mick Kubarkku's *Mimi Spirit* (left) is a very ancient form. The artist is from Yikarrakkal country in the Northern Territory, and has produced a huge oeuvre since the 1970s.

Performances involving dance and song are popularly known as 'corroborees'. The dancers are prepared by being painted and decorated, then they emerge onto the dancing ground from behind a screen of branches, accompanied by singing and rhythmic clapping of hands and boomerangs. The lead singer will begin a verse, and a chorus will then repeat his words in a song-dialogue known as 'tracking':

> At Rarrdjali
> The sun rises
> and a bird sings:
> 'djiburr-djiburr'

The sequence finishes with a trill on the boomerangs and a vigorous 'Ee-ya!' from all the participants. The dancers retire to their shelter at this point, to re-emerge when the singing starts up again with the next verse. A range of corroborees take this general form, but there are sacred ones restricted to men or women only, and there are more public ones that have been created by gifted singers. These poets will usually attribute the inspiration to a kind of spirit, or to the ghost of a dead relative who comes to them in a dream. Little children are encouraged to participate in these public corroborees.

The destiny of the Indigenous 'tribes' was forged as soon as the Europeans arrived with a *terra nullius* mentality. Impelled by the imperatives of colonization and development, they saw the country as a virgin land for their taking. The Indigenous peoples were chased off their lands, marginalized, and even poisoned and massacred. At the beginning of the 20th century their numbers were seriously diminished and they became an invisible people.

CHAPTER 3

AN EMPTY LAND?

If Australia, a vast and open country (right), was supposed to be 'free' for colonization, the irony is that exploration and subsequent economic development would simply not have been possible without both the co-operation and exploitation of the Indigenous peoples (opposite), who in the process lost their lands and their freedom.

Appropriation

At the time of the first British settlement in 1788, there were perhaps one million Aboriginal people living on the continent. They occupied almost every corner of the land mass, and lived in more than five hundred tribal groupings, each with its own language, or at least dialect. Yet, despite the clear presence of Indigenous people, the colonizers came to believe, and to justify their actions by the belief, that the land was unused and therefore available. Seeing no evidence of 'sovereign power', the British explorers claimed territory for their Crown. The 1788 settlement confirmed this assertion of British sovereignty over 'New South Wales' as then understood and eventually the claim came to cover all of modern Australia.

GOVERNOR DAVEY'S PROCLAMATION TO THE ABORIGINES 1816.

"Why Massa Gobernor", said Black Jack – "Um Proclamation all gammon"
"Bin Blackfellow read him eh? So no learn him read book."
"Read that then" said the Governor, pointing to a picture.

This claim to exclusive sovereignty required British and later colonial governments to set up various landholding arrangements: freehold ownership, leasehold and reserves of various kinds. The details of these arrangements have often been of great importance to Aboriginal people, especially in recent years. In general, though, and particularly in the richest farming areas, the Indigenous inhabitants were pushed off the land, often with extreme violence. They either fled or were forced into settlements run by missionaries and by governments – there was frequently little difference. Relatively few Indigenous people (mainly those in central and northern Australia) managed to stay on or near their ancestral lands.

From about 1820 Australia stopped being seen by the Old World as its antipodean gaol, and more as a new land of opportunity, *Australia Felix*. It saw more and

This proclamation (above) was posted in 1829 by Governor George Arthur to illustrate reciprocal care and the illegality of violence between the races. While this ideal was rarely practised, it is significant that colonial violence was always tempered by a humanitarian impulse on the part of many clergymen and Christian organizations.

more free settlers arriving, occupying more lands in remote areas and extending pastoralism (in 1838 there were three million sheep), growing grain crops and later mining. The need for a workforce again accelerated immigration from Britain and Ireland. Between 1830 and 1840, some 170,000 settlers embarked for Australia. The territorial occupation proceeded anarchically as free settlers known as squatters took up vast tracts of land semi-legally, chasing off the Indigenous owners by force. When Aborigines had helped themselves to cattle or sheep, or attacked a settler for whatever reason, retaliatory violence was justified either on the grounds of the 'treachery of the savages' (who were no doubt defending their ancestral lands and their people) or on the grounds of property.

Indigenous guides

However the Europeans did depend on Indigenous knowledge, as guides often led pioneers into unknown country, showing them the tracks and water sources, bush food and good camping sites. These hardy pioneers would then unreflectingly claim to be the 'first people'

Before the act of annexation in the late 18th century, the British government warned its colonists to avoid conflict with Indigenous peoples. But the ethnocentrism and prior assumptions of the invaders made it hard for them to recognize the Aboriginal lifestyle as 'civilized'. Enclosing and cultivating land for agriculture was paramount in the minds of the settlers and they imposed strict discipline on Indigenous workers, with little understanding of the spiritual practices that tied these peoples to their lands. Below, a photo of 1855 shows a pioneer couple surrounded by Aborigines.

to have discovered a particular place, and then endow it with the name of an English lord. For them the invisibility of the Indigenous peoples was necessary to achieve their own aims. This invisibility was more sustained at the level of official ideology, and less among the people. In everyday life, colonists frequently had close relationships with Aboriginal people: as work-mates, friends, sexual partners, sometimes spouses. Such relationships emerged of necessity in the colonists' adaptation to the new country. For their part, while Aborigines had tried to drive out the invaders early on, they later hoped to assimilate the new arrivals to their way of life. These were complex relationships of interdependence, and as the numbers of colonists grew to proportions that overpowered those of the indigenes, the assimilation started to occur in the other direction.

The settlement of Australia could not have even begun without Aboriginal guides. Their role was later forgotten by a generation of historians who celebrated, in the language of 'first discovery', the heroics of the nation-building explorers. As the first Europeans blundered through bush country, the Aborigines, skilled trackers and expert bushmen, moved through it with ease, and showed the explorers where to go and how to obtain water. These explorers were not conquering a wilderness, but moving through country that had been occupied for generations and shaped by firestick farming. In desert country L. H. Wells admitted that 'without a guide in such country one is almost powerless' and he captured and chained Aborigines to force them to lead his party to water. Thus, throughout the country, roads came to be made and settlements established along the traditional tracks and in the good places that had been shown to the settlers by the local black inhabitants.

This was just a start. As the settlers began to bring their sheep and cattle, and to fence the country to create their own ideal economic units, they discovered that they still could not dispense with Aboriginal help. This was a complex situation. Aborigines were obviously not happy about being mistreated and moved off their ancestral lands, and they saw the appearance of livestock as a handy and easily speared resource.

The pioneers built rudimentary huts (below right, Victoria, 1905) and paddocks (above right) to show their possession of the land. Many Indigenous families also took up agriculture. At the end of the 19th century, historian Heather Goodall tells us, two Koori families in New South Wales had converted country originally classified as 'suitable for grazing only' into 'suitable for cultivation': 'In only two years, the Davis and Mosely families at Euroka had cleared and cropped 17 acres with maize, planted fruit trees and vegetables and begun raising chickens. By 1899 their maize crop had yielded 800 bushels.' They built barns for their produce and 'comfortable slab and bark dwellings' for themselves. As they later argued, the Moselys and Davises had transformed the lands into 'very desirable farms without any assistance from the government.' But their success lasted only a few years: the government intervened and turned their land into a reserve for other Aborigines.

The discovery of gold in Victoria and NSW in 1851 caused a rush of immigrants. In ten years the population of settlers trebled to 1.2 million souls.

'The only way to survive in this wild country was to show who was master'

The Indigenous resistance was very localized but also determined. And it eventually was stopped by some of the most brutal and lawless paramilitary forces in the history of the country, the Native Police corps, first raised in Queensland in 1848, to 'clear the country' and subdue Indigenous uprisings. By the 1870s there were about two hundred of these mounted Black Australian soldiers roaming the colony with a white commander, travelling up to fifty kilometres a day, opening fire on any people they encountered. Women and children were not exempt. A white lieutenant, Frederick Wheeler, who had shot dead an innocent ten-year-old child with white witnesses present, told a government committee: 'I act on my own discretion, and on my own responsibility',

Police forces with Aboriginal troopers existed in several states in the 19th century. These Aborigines assisted in applying the settlers' law, and were often recruited from other areas and so had no ties to the people they were subjecting. In 1859, Queensland became a separate colony and the Native Mounted Police unit of 22 white officers and 120 Aboriginal troopers was formed. The frontiers were patrolled by groups of about eight, fully

and walked out of the room. The commanders even shot their own troops if they wanted to. They did not take prisoners or report the names and numbers of people they executed. Women they kept for their own purposes.

equipped with Snider rifles. The force was abandoned in 1900. In 1888 a special force (above) was recruited to hunt for the outlaw Ned Kelly in Victoria.

Pastoralists joined forces with the troops whenever they were needed, since they wanted to protect their pastoral investments against the 'inferior race'. Late in the 19th century, a regional newspaper in the far north of Western Australia published a letter from a settler: 'It would be a good time for the Western Australian government…to shut its eyes for say three months and let the settlers up here have a little time to teach the nigger the difference between thine and mine…it would only have to be done once and once done could easily be forgotten about.'

He and his neighbours were afraid, no doubt, of 'wild blackfellas' because of reports that they were regularly spearing the invaders' cattle as they tried to settle the country. This letter is also evidence of how some settlers took the law into their own hands and 'dispersed' any blacks they found on the country they wished to occupy.

The involvement of Indigenous Australians in the Native Mounted Police, often against their will, led to the death and imprisonment of thousands of other Aborigines. However, exposure to firearms and to military training also enabled the First Australians to mount some of the fiercest armed rebellions against white incursions, such as the Tjandamara uprisings of the 1890s.

In Tasmania in the early 19th century, settlers were pushing Aborigines off their traditional hunting grounds. Aborigines replied to this treatment by raiding isolated farms (above). In 1830 the Big River tribe killed twenty settlers, and in that year the notorious 'black line' of whites attempted to drive the Aborigines to one peninsula, but only one old man and a child were captured. The last few Aborigines agreed to depart to an island off the coast, and in 1876 Trugannini, one of the most famous Tasmanian Aboriginal women, died. Her bones were placed on show at a museum, until her descendants were able to give her an honourable burial in 1976.

Pigeon the Bushranger and the Kalkatungu Revolt

In this context, a now-celebrated figure emerged, one whose mythology joins that of the historical figures of the Australian 'bushrangers', the outlaws of the early years of the colony. Tjandamara, or 'Pigeon' began working for the police as a tracker, leading them to Aborigines who were spearing cattle. Suddenly he had a change of heart, releasing his countrymen, killing the police and making off with the arms and ammunition. He and his gang of warriors were responsible for killing many whites over the next decade, raiding settlers' homesteads and ambushing them on the road.

The Kalkatungu were a large nation of about 2,000 people prior to invasion, occupying some thousands of square kilometres around what is the now the mining town of Mount Isa in north-west Queensland. The rugged terrain of their country, like Pigeon's, provided many natural hiding places. However water was not abundant, and this made it even more urgent for them to conserve their resources against the intrusions of the white man. Their resistance was carried out between 1874 and 1884. While the Kalkatungu initially had tactical advantages in their knowledge of the terrain, and their intelligence about enemy movements, their weapons were in the end no match for the firearms of the troopers. The final confrontation with the Kalkatungu was in 1884 after years of guerrilla ambushes and white retaliations. Two hundred Native Police rode out to the hills to confront about six hundred Kalkatungu warriors painted up for battle and ranged on the side of the mountain, now known as Battle Mountain. Many Kalkatungu died in the uneven contest.

'Pacification'

Relations between colonists and Indigenous peoples were not always confrontational. After initial attempts to scare off the invaders, the locals deployed various strategies to accommodate them to their way of life, but in the end the process went more rapidly in the other direction.

As regions became 'pacified', beginning with the south-east corner of the continent, the remaining

Traditional tribesmen, rounded up and put on the chain for crimes as minor as killing cattle (above), were often sent 2,000 km south by boat to Rottnest Island near Perth. Here, in the cold and far from their home country, few survived to tell their tale, much less find a way home again.

Indigenous peoples learnt the skills of farming, worked for white people, and made efforts to establish their own farming ventures, battling the strong opposition from the settlers who sought to keep the 'natives in their place' and out of the economy. The skills and abilities of the Aborigines were readily acknowledged (a local magistrate wrote back to England that it was 'wonderful to see how readily the bush natives can comprehend and adapt themselves'). But skills and labour were resources to be harnessed as cheaply as possible, at the same time as the

At the beginning of the 20th century, a German missionary was of the opinion that any racial mixing was a danger to Australia's future, and recommended that Aborigines be placed in protected zones to avoid all contact with the whites.

basis of the traditional culture and economy was destroyed. Complex relationships of interdependence were established as Indigenous Australians participated in the rapid transformation of their own country, and white Australians found themselves subtly but profoundly influenced by the Indigenous way of life.

Life among the cattle

At any one time from 1900 to the 1960s there were about 10,000 Aborigines working in the cattle industry in Northern Australia. The minimal recompense they received enabled pastoralists to save about £50 a year for each black worker. Some properties were the size of small countries and were owned by overseas interests. Effectively, the Aboriginal workers' labour ensured the viability of the industries and the wealth of the owners. For the Aborigines there were some advantages to living the tough life of the cowboy. They were able to stay in their own country and visit its sacred places, and they were able to gain some respect and self-satisfaction in mastering an aspect of the introduced culture.

But the treatment of Aboriginal people was frequently inhumane. They could be traded like chattels. Stations were sold at a higher price if they were 'well-stocked' with

Jack Sullivan was part-Aboriginal and became head stockman on the Duracks' stations. He recalls: 'Breaking in horses and mules was a white man's job, and by and by when yellow fellers [i.e. part-Indigenous] got experience they could do it too. In those days there were not big wages. I started off with thirty bob a week …blackfellas didn't get anything as yet, only the white men and the yellow fellers…Being a head stockman meant that you had a hold of the game and had a station team young enough to do the work.'

Aborigines. Young boys and girls were vulnerable and unprotected. In the Kimberley, Mary Durack tells us: '...the eight-year-old Boxer had come across from Queensland with his mother and a man called Wesley Lyttleton, then on their way to the Halls Creek goldfields. Pumpkin, so the story goes, took a fancy to the boy and

acquired him in exchange for a good packhorse and a tin of jam.'

Boxer went on to be highly respected in both white and black communities; he was both very capable and very lucky. Others were shot, beaten or abused. Young girls became housemaids and, if not looked after by the mistress, the concubines of the men on the station. As Henry Reynolds put it: 'Young Aboriginal girls were universally considered to be fair fucking game by "the boss", his sons, the Chinese cook or indeed anyone who had half a chance to "bust a young gin".'

In the north-west and the Torres Strait, the pearling industry was booming from the beginning of the 20th century. Aborigines were 'run down' in the bush and dragged in on chains to work diving for pearl shell, opening and cleaning it and then packing it for transport. This dangerous and labour-intensive work was often paid for in food and tobacco.

Until the 1960s, many Aboriginal people in northern Australia worked for rations or as unpaid labour in rural industries. The strategies employed to secure the workers also included a kind of moral disciplinary training in missions, as well as strange edicts like that issued by Governor Hutt of Western Australia, that 'no Aborigines could enter Perth unless they were wearing woollen shirts which had to be "earned by labour".' Meanwhile, the challenge of simply gaining employment was one of the greatest obstacles faced by Indigenous people.

The politics of racial assimilation

The federation of the Australian colonies in 1901 meant that Australia as a nation was officially born. At the time this happened with pomp and ceremony in Melbourne, there were significant numbers of Indigenous people living in the remoter parts of Australia who were not only living their lives in their own land as their ancestors always had, but could not speak English and had never heard the word 'Australia'. The Fathers of Federation did not think to invite a representative to the very ceremony that excluded any possibility of Indigenous sovereignty.

The newly-adopted federal Constitution led to a peculiar exclusion. Since representation in the Parliament was linked to the population as determined by census, and since the number of Aborigines in remote areas could not be accurately determined, all Indigenous people were excluded from the census. Only those Indigenous individuals already permitted to vote in their former colony in 1900 and 1901 were allowed their democratic rights. This injustice, so typical of the pervasive racial prejudice through most of Australian history, was not removed until 1967.

The new Commonwealth continued the uprooting of Indigenous peoples by placing them forcefully in missions or reserves where they were restricted in their ability to hunt, practise their traditional ceremonies,

The first Aboriginal cricket team went to Britain in 1868, a decade before the first white team. The tour was highly successful, with the team winning many games in the country of the sport's origin. Young Nannultera (above) was thus one of the first to distinguish himself in an imported sport, and many of his countrymen and women were subsequently to prove themselves fine athletes. It was a test for the assimilation that became government policy only much later, with mixed results.

and be married without permission, and where they were subjected to food rationing and a curfew. One of its most pernicious and damaging outcomes was that Aboriginal children in their thousands were forcibly removed from their parents without their consent (often by local police) and were placed in orphanages or were sent to live with white families as domestic servants, right through until the 1960s. Government officials justified these heart-rending practices by claiming that they were instituted for Aboriginal children 'for their own good'. Some were no doubt saved from poverty or worse, but the policy as a whole was part of a eugenicist logic of assimilation.

The civilizing work of missions

In 1912 the Worora people watched a group of Presbyterian missionaries anchor their lugger, land, and prepare to establish a mission. One of the leaders, Ambula, yelled at his people to kill them. 'No,' urged some others, 'They are not trying to harm us. They do not hunt our food. They have given us food and gifts. We have nothing to fear from them.' There was nothing to fear except the white man's version of civilization.

The first missionaries arrived in NSW and Western Australia in about 1821, then spread to the other states. Missions did in fact save many groups who might otherwise have perished in fringe camps around towns, subject to the worst influences of frontier life and racist abuse. But there was also a price to pay. In many missions – Catholic, Lutheran, Anglican – there were concerted

In Victoria in 1863, a group of Aboriginal people from the Kulin nation tired of waiting for the government to choose a new reserve for them and settled on land that would become known as Coranderrk Station. Later, the government began to send more people there. Those who settled at Coranderrk (below) intended to look after themselves by farming and educating their own children, but by 1924 it was closed. In 1998, Coranderrk land was purchased by the Indigenous Land Corporation and returned to Aboriginal people.

attempts to stamp out 'primitive practices' like the initiation of young men, which often took the form of circumcision. Traditional languages and ceremonies were also forbidden. This was the cultural arm of the colonial endeavour; Christianity eventually touched the lives of nearly the whole Indigenous population. While adults were sometimes considered a lost cause, attempts were made to segregate the children in dormitories and to inculcate the precepts of the Bible. The regimentation and cruelty held little attraction for children used to the warmth and laughter of their own homes.

When the Benedictines set up a mission in the far north of the Kimberleys in 1908, they did not see a local Aborigine for four years: 'They hung presents and food in the trees and these gifts were taken, but no contact was made until 1912.' There was a little more success in the southern parts of Australia where Aborigines were more quickly outnumbered and moved from their lands to missions where they were protected from some of the worst effects of white settler racism. In the early 20th

century at Point McLeay mission in South Australia, important members of the community were converted to Christianity and became lay preachers like James Unaipon and his son, David, but others expressed their resistance. A character called Tommy Walker, who had espoused drink rather than God, attended Holy Communion at Point McLeay and 'drained the cup eagerly and cried out boldly, "Fill 'im up again!"' Missionaries had great difficulty translating Christian concepts into the local languages. At one mission Aborigines sang for years 'Jesus loves hair on the chest' instead of 'Jesus loves me'. Clearly the missionary was pointing to his chest and suggesting the word for 'me', and had become the victim of the kind of practical joke for which Aboriginal people

The missions served to supplant Aboriginal cultures through religious conversion, 'civilize' children through education (above), and provide some substitute for a lost community life.

are famous, and which represented a mode of joyful resistance.

Towards the end of the 19th century, state governments, through their so-called Protectors of Aborigines and their Departments of Native Welfare, had almost total control over the Aboriginal population. While occasionally some people may have been protected from the excesses of racist violence, the lack of freedom to enjoy one's own culture, or participate in one's own economy, combined with a lack of citizenship rights and responsibilities meant that Indigenous Australians were caught in a double bind: urged to be 'the same', but always treated as if they were 'not ready yet'. This was the faulty logic of 'assimilation'. In any case, right up until about 1965, most white Australians were convinced that they were overseeing the demise of an inferior race and culture, and that Aboriginal people were simply unable to adapt and prosper in white society. In 1906 Bishop Frodsham declared: 'In the course of a generation or two, at the most, the last Australian blackfellow will have turned his face to warm mother earth....'

Aborigines were not predisposed to worship a single god, and their own beliefs made them cherish life in the here and now. Yet when thrown together in missions (above) and dislocated from their ancestral lands, they began to talk, in the south-east of the continent, of a god called Baiami who, some said, 'dwells in heaven on a throne of transparent crystal surrounded by beautifully carved pillars from which emanate the colours of the rainbow.' This syncretic vision emerged in the absence of sacred rituals, which could not be performed without visiting the sacred places.

In a 1967 referendum, Australians voted overwhelmingly to change their country's constitution. As a result, for the first time, all Indigenous Australians were counted in the federal census and came under the legislative protection of the Commonwealth government. But it was not until 1993 – in the wake of the 1992 Mabo decision by the High Court of Australia – that the possibility of Native Title was formally recognized by the federal Parliament. After two hundred years of denial, Indigenous people across the nation were finally able to begin to obtain legislative recognition of their rights to land.

CHAPTER 4

WE HAVE SURVIVED!

The Aboriginal flag (right) was designed in 1972 by Harold Thomas. Black is for the colour of the skin; red represents the desert sands and the blood spilt in the struggles for freedom; yellow is the sun, which is the source of all life. Opposite, a didjeridu player amid the 'Sea of Hands', a symbol of reconciliation.

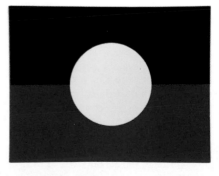

Growing political awareness

From the late 1930s until the 1970s, all state and federal governments supported and enforced assimilation policies designed to take as many First Australians as possible away from their distinctive identity. They felt that an Aborigine should be indistinguishable in every way from 'every other Australian'; not an Aborigine at all.

One response to this assimilationist agenda was the mobilization of Indigenous political groups. The first formal Aboriginal protest group to be formed in New South Wales, the Aborigines' Progressive Association (APA) both resisted the dictates of white Australian society and collaborated with individual white Australian allies, such as the publisher and critic P. R. Stephensen. Political groups multiplied, often in collaboration with the trade unions, certain members of the Australian Labor Party and even the Communist Party. These protest movements culminated in the 'Day of Mourning' organized by the Australian Aborigines' League (AAL) and the APA on 26 January 1938. The event deplored the sesquicentennial of the British occupation of Australia at exactly the moment when official commemorative celebrations were taking place in the city of Sydney and at Botany Bay. Key Indigenous leaders of the APA, William Ferguson and Jack Patten also co-wrote a manifesto entitled 'Aborigines Claim Citizenship Rights', one of the seminal documents in Australian Aboriginal history. Its opening words were as surprising as they were uncompromising: 'This festival of 150 years' so-called "progress" in Australia commemorates also 150 years of misery and degradation imposed upon the original native inhabitants by the white invaders of this country.'

The consequences of the Second World War

These political movements were interrupted by the global crisis of the Second World War. It clearly was one

In this famous photograph (below) are the main players in the 'Day of Mourning' protest, the first national political demonstration in defence of Indigenous Australian rights. From left to right: William Ferguson, Jack Kinchela, Helen Grosvenor, and (at front right) Selina and Jack Patten. In his speech, Patten listed the many injustices that his people had endured and demanded equal rights, including full citizenship. More than a thousand Aborigines from every state in Australia – men, women and children – came to take part in the protest rally. Pamphlets distributed in reserves and country towns made it clear that the event was restricted to 'Aborigines Only' – another significant form of independent assertiveness.

of the most influential events in Indigenous Australian history over the past 50 years. More than 1,000 people of Aboriginal descent (including a separate battalion of around 740 Torres Strait Islanders) fought in the Australian forces in the war. In addition, a group of about 50 Black Australians – the Northern Territory Special Reconnaissance Unit – was mobilized under the leadership of the anthropologist Donald Thomson to repel the potential Japanese invasion of Arnhem Land. In fact, all of these First Australians were effectively invisible, since official military policy at the time forbade the conscription of Aborigines. These soldiers received just a fraction of the wages paid to non-Aboriginal soldiers; members of the special Arnhem Land unit only received three sticks of tobacco per week!

From 1944 onwards, many of the so-called 'Black Diggers' came home to become vocal critics of the military for its exploitation of Indigenous soldiers.

The Torres Strait Islander Battalion (below) were paid with weekly rations during World War II. They were not compensated with military pensions until the 1980s. Captain Reg Saunders, from Portland, Victoria, was the first Indigenous soldier to become a commissioned officer.

They did not get war pensions or other benefits due to regular soldiers. Several became spokespeople for the broader Aboriginal and Torres Strait Islander cause.

Anglo-Australia and post-war migration

At the end of the Second World War, Australia was remarkably homogeneous in ethnic and cultural terms. The infamous White Australia immigration policy, which had been in place for half a century, had done its job. At that time, more than 70 per cent of Australia's population of 7.4 million traced its heritage to the United Kingdom. Australia was as British as it would ever be.

At the close of the war there was also a severe shortage of labour, so a 'populate or perish' policy was put in place by the federal government, broadening the migration net to include the countries of Western and Eastern Europe, while still preserving a strong bias towards the United Kingdom. By the late 1950s, hundreds of thousands of

In the immediate post-war period, the Australian authorities adopted many policies that exclusively encouraged Caucasian immigration. Advertising campaigns promoting 'White Australia' (photograph above) were common, aided by financial incentives. In 1948, Arthur Calwell, the federal Minister for Immigration, famously declared that – as far as the country's immigration future was concerned – 'Two Wongs do not make a White'.

migrants from Italy, Greece, Yugoslavia, the Netherlands, Germany, France and many other European countries had arrived on Australian shores.

However, in 1961, Australia was still indisputably dominated by its expatriate British culture. In many ways, the Australia of that era is hard to recollect or to imagine for those living in the country just four decades later. All the major social forces of the late 20th century – the women's movement, the environmental lobby, the civil rights and peace movements – were yet to make their mark. The nation was still under the profound influence of Australia's longest-serving Prime Minister, the conservative royalist Sir Robert Menzies. Australia's national currency of pounds, shillings and pence echoed that of Great Britain; the metric system was still to come; and the divide between Catholics and Protestants was still fundamental. School children still sang 'God Save the Queen' at assemblies, prominent Australians still received peerages from the Crown and most (often financially assisted) immigrants came from the British Isles.

The sea-change in the forty years that followed 1961 is almost unimaginable. In 1972 the White Australia policy was finally officially repealed; as that decade continued, refugees from the war in Vietnam joined migrants from all over the world to a vastly liberalized Australia. By the early 1990s, more than 5 million migrants had settled in Australia, doubling the country's post-war population. Today, well in excess of 40 per cent of Australia's population of 20 million people are either post-1946 migrants, their children or grandchildren, and the fastest-growing migrant source nations are those of South-East Asia and the Middle East.

The Indigenous situation

What was the situation for Aboriginal people at this time? In 1961 the official federal government policy of assimilation still held sway. For example, a 'Native

As this cover of *Bulletin* magazine from 1996 illustrates (below), the policy of multiculturalism has been a cornerstone of Australian life since its introduction in 1973. Other policies introduced by the reformist government of Labor Prime Minister Gough Whitlam from 1972 to 1975 included the formation of an Australian Council for the Arts, the creation of a Department of Aboriginal Affairs and the establishment of an Australian Council for Ethnic Affairs. Later governments (such as the administration of Liberal Prime Minister Malcolm Fraser, 1975–83) enhanced multiculturalism via the creation of a Special Broadcasting Service, for multilingual radio and television broadcasts.

Welfare Conference' of that year defined assimilation as follows: 'all Aborigines and part-Aborigines are expected eventually to attain the same manner of living as other Australians and to live as members of a single Australian community, enjoying the same rights and privileges, accepting the same responsibilities, observing the same customs and influenced by the same beliefs, hopes and loyalties as other Australians.'

This famous policy pronouncement revealed so much. First, it assumed that there was a 'single Australian community' to which one could aspire in the first place, with coherently similar 'customs, beliefs, hopes and loyalties'. But there was more.

The additional point, and a key theme in Aboriginal history, is that very specific, local issues coalesce with international forces, with both focusing intensely upon Indigenous Australians. Aboriginal issues are – simultaneously – some of the most insistently local and international questions affecting all Australians. The assimilation debate is just one example. While it was

A boriginal people – even those based in the cities – acknowledge the importance of connection with their traditional communities. Senior women (below) are often crucial to the cultural continuum and take leading roles in legal aid, housing, health and other Indigenous organizations throughout the country.

held out as a beacon of cultural uniformity for Aborigines at the local or community level, it also was held up as an underpinning aim of Australia's international migration policy: both were intended to effect an embrace of the 'Australian way of life'.

The long march towards recognition of rights

Aborigines and Torres Strait Islanders have often found themselves positioned on the bridge between the global and the local. In many cases, the global issues have been thrust upon them. However, there are others in which Indigenous Australians have made a conscious decision to enter the international arena, to emulate overseas action and to respond to challenges on their own terms.

In 1944 Aborigines were allowed to become "Australian Citizens." Aboriginal people called their citizenship papers "Dog Tags." We had to be licensed to be called Australian.

Significantly, in 1961, Joe McGuiness was elected the first Aboriginal president of the Federal Council for the Advancement of Aborigines and Torres Strait Islanders (FCAATSI). The members of FCAATSI had a number of aims: to get equal pay and the right to manage their own communities and to end social and political discrimination. One can see direct, inspirational links between the efforts of FCAATSI and of the National Association for the Advancement of Colored People (NAACP) in the United States during the same era. One can also see the clear influence of the American Civil Rights movement upon the 1965 campaign of Freedom Rides that took place in Australia. Here, a coalition of non-Aboriginal university students and young Aboriginal leaders like Charles Perkins were involved in non-violent protest action directed against segregation and injustice in small towns in northern New South Wales. There was also overwhelming public support for the federal referendum of 1967 (in which more than 90 per cent of the Australian electorate voted for constitutional change affecting Indigenous people). The resultant reforms – such as the enumeration of Aboriginal people in the national census and the extension of federal legislative protection by the Commonwealth government – were

This ironic and iconic poster, entitled *Citizenship* (above), was designed in 1987 by the Indigenous novelist and artist Sally Morgan. It represents the infamous Exemption Certificate (colloquially known as a 'Dog Collar' or 'Dog Tag') introduced in the 1940s. This government certificate gave partial citizenship rights (such as the franchise) to certain Aboriginal people on the understanding that they renounced allegedly 'primitive' aspects of their culture, cut ties with traditional communities and adopted the 'customs of civilized life'. These certificates were actually considered to be an enlightened policy measure at the time.

arguably influenced by the growing worldwide trend towards decolonization.

The same year of 1967 saw the most sustained and significant strike by Aboriginal pastoral workers in the Northern Territory, when the Gurindji people 'walked off' Wave Hill Station to protest against inequalities in working and living conditions. It was the first Aboriginal land rights bid in modern Australian history to also use industrial action. Ultimately, they too were successful.

The Yolngu people from the Northern Territory were land-rights pioneers. The Gove Land Rights case (1971) pitted mining interests against native title and paved the way for later recognition of Indigenous rights. Earlier, in 1963, a highly innovative bark petition, combining a text in English with traditional Yolngu art, was a powerful expression of political will.

The 1970s

In the early 1970s, the formation of an Australian Black Power group, led by Aboriginal activists such as Gary Foley and Denis Walker, was clearly inspired by the American Black Panther movement. Its aims were insistently directed at other Australians, in Foley's words: 'The Australian Government has reduced Aboriginals to

In February 1965 a bus full of Indigenous students and their white supporters began a trip of several weeks through rural New South Wales, protesting against the racial discrimination that existed in clubs, pubs and swimming pools. Known as the Freedom Ride, and led by Charles Perkins, it became a key event in the contemporary Indigenous struggle, partly because it received intense local and international media attention.

the same level as flora and fauna by saying we belong to the land, but the land doesn't belong to us. We want land rights now and then the black man can assimilate, integrate or live separately. But he must be able to choose for himself.'

All of this internationally inspired activity was transformed at the local level. Just as country music performed in Nashville was emulated, and then altered, by Aboriginal musicians in Tamworth in New South Wales, these social movements and trends were 'Aboriginalized' by, and for, the benefit of Indigenous Australians. It was not a matter of copying foreign ways but of the strategic use of selected international ideas, which were then adapted to suit local cultures, purposes and aims.

Revolution in a tent

A case in point was the erection of the Aboriginal Tent Embassy on the lawns of Parliament House in Canberra on 27 January 1972. This ingenious political protest was brilliantly symbolic. Trading upon the fact that Australia's capital city was home to more than a hundred foreign diplomatic missions, the Embassy reinforced the image

The arrival in power of the Labor Prime Minister Gough Whitlam marked a watershed in Australian political life. Whitlam began by disengaging Australia from the war in Vietnam. He then led reforms to the system of social and medical security, which resulted in a universal health care scheme called Medicare. He is also credited with establishing a dialogue with Aboriginal and Torres Strait Islander peoples and with responding to public protests for land rights (above). In 1975, during his second term in office, a Racial Discrimination Act was passed, which prohibited any legislative or individual action that was discriminatory on the basis of race, colour, national or ethnic origin.

of Aborigines as being citizens without their own nation: foreigners in their own land. The impact was electric. One of the most prominent activists of the era, Roberta Sykes commented: 'The Embassy was a black affair; it wasn't blacks being guided by whites...it was the first national announcement that the pushing back was going to stop.'

The Embassy also invoked the stark social and medical statistics that afflicted (and still afflict) Aboriginal Australians. Just as their tent symbolized the fact that they were, in relative terms, paupers, to this day Indigenous Australians suffer by far the worst health, mortality and incarceration rates of all Australian citizens. Today, the Aboriginal Embassy remains in the grounds opposite the Old Parliament House in Canberra. It has expanded from its humble canvas beginnings to embrace a larger site, a permanent fire, and a permanent protest. But until the conditions affecting Aboriginal people are redressed in terms of health, education and opportunity, and until there is real recognition of Indigenous nationhood, the Embassy will remain. And the 'revolution that began in a tent' will continue.

The establishment of the Tent Embassy (opposite) in 1972 was an historic moment in the Aboriginal struggle for recognition. Since that time, that modest structure has grown, been torn down by the police, been transformed and has evolved into a permanent site of protest. Attempts to remove the Embassy have failed: in July 2002 the local government attempted to cut its electricity supply in the coldest month of the Canberra winter; within hours, Greenpeace Australia had offered the protesters solar energy panels as a replacement.

Legal recognition of land ownership

The progressive Labor government of Gough Whitlam was elected in 1972 and moved very fast on the Indigenous political issues that had been gaining strength. By 1975 the symbolic gesture of a handful of red earth and the title deeds to Gurindji land hit the headlines. The same year a Ministry of Aboriginal Affairs was created, and then eight years later two other important bodies: the Aboriginal Development Commission, with the task of funding community activities, and the National

Aboriginal Conference of elected Indigenous representatives, as well as local Land Councils in each region. Charles Perkins, a senior bureaucrat, was behind many of these initiatives.

1976 saw the signing of the Aboriginal Land Rights (Northern Territory) Act, which enabled the transfer of some Crown land or former reserves to Indigenous control. More meaningful forms of Indigenous ownership were developed. Since that time, the situation across the continent has remained inconsistent and heavily politicized, but extensive areas are now under various forms of Indigenous ownership and custodianship. Country with little pastoral or agricultural potential has sometimes proven to contain valuable minerals; traditional Indigenous owners can negotiate for royalties or to be stakeholders in developments. This has resulted in positive social developments, especially in Arnhem Land.

The Mabo case

A major legal change came in June 1992 when, by a majority decision, the High Court of Australia ruled on behalf of the Indigenous claimants in the Mabo case. Eddie Mabo was a member of the Meriam people, the traditional owners of Murray Island and surrounding islands and reefs in the Torres Strait. The islands in the Strait were

In 1966, Vincent Lingiari, one of the elders of the Gurindji mob on Wave Hill Station in the Northern Territory, led a famous strike against atrocious wages and conditions. But the real struggle was for land, and it took nine years, with Lingiari apparently saying to an offer from the absentee English landlord, Lord Vestey, 'You can keep your gold, we just want our land back'. In 1975, in a celebrated moment (opposite below), Gough Whitlam started a land rights process he was unable to finish, as he announced: 'Vincent Lingiari, I solemnly hand to you these deeds as proof, in Australian law, that these lands belong to the Gurindji people and I put into your hands part of the earth itself as a sign that this land will be the possession of you and your children forever.'

annexed as part of the colony of Queensland in 1879. In 1982, Mabo and four other Islanders commenced legal action against the Queensland state government in support of the traditional land rights of the Meriam. Their position was that the Islanders had inhabited and possessed their lands continuously and that they had lived in permanent communities with their own social and political organization. On 3 June 1992, the High Court upheld the Islanders' claim. This could not overturn the sovereignty of the Australian government, nor the ownership of lands now held privately, but it did open the way for title to Crown lands or national parks to be challenged by traditional owners.

Unfortunately, this watershed legal decision raised high hopes that were not fulfilled in the decade that followed. To date, very few Indigenous claims to land have been upheld by the various Native Title Tribunals created in 1993 in the legislative aftermath of the Mabo decision. Meanwhile, millions of dollars have been spent on legal arguments, challenges and interpretations. One outcome has been a tendency for corporate interests, such as mining companies, to negotiate directly with Indigenous claimants to avoid the tortuous Native Title process. The widely acclaimed Cape York Land Use Agreement negotiated in 1998 by Indigenous lawyer Noel Pearson and others is a key example.

Each of the major Indigenous tribal groups or communities has a Land Council whose job is to present cases to the National Native Title Tribunal, the judicial body charged with making such determinations. Since it was created in 1993, it has considered hundreds of cases, but only a small number have been decided in favour of the Indigenous claimants.

From Reconciliation to Olympics

The last ten years has seen the pursuit of a national agenda of Reconciliation between Aboriginal and non-Aboriginal Australians. Again, this signals the intersection between international forces (such as the Truth and Reconciliation Commission in South Africa) and the particular circumstances of Indigenous Australia. The Reconciliation theme has been widely and popularly embraced: the most significant public demonstrations in support of the Reconciliation agenda occurred around Australia in May 2000. In Australia's most populous city, Sydney, more than 250,000 people took part in the

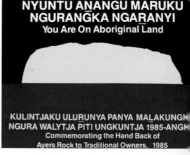

NYUNTU ANANGU MARUKU NGURANGKA NGARANYI
You Are On Aboriginal Land

KULINTJAKU ULURUNYA PANYA MALAKUNGK
NGURA WALYTJA PITI UNGKUNTJA 1985-ANGK
Commemorating the Hand Back of
Ayers Rock to Traditional Owners, 1985

This poster from 1985, in the colours of the Aboriginal flag, commemorates the return of the sacred site at Ayers Rock to the local owners, who have put its original name Uluru back into currency.

largest peaceful demonstration in Australia's history as they walked across Sydney Harbour Bridge.

The symbolism of a 'potentially reconciled' Australia was lent further impetus when Sydney hosted the 2000 Summer Olympic Games. From the highlights of Indigenous history and religion that featured in the opening ceremony to the lighting of the Olympic torch by Indigenous athlete Cathy Freeman, Aboriginal and Torres Strait Islander people took centre-stage in this mammoth international event. Throughout the Games – which included Freeman's gold-medal triumph in the 400 metres as well as impressive performances by other Indigenous athletes such as Kyle Vander-Kuyp, Patrick Johnson and Nova Peris – Aboriginal Australia was the underlying theme. To further emphasize this point of reconciling with history, during the Games' closing ceremony the popular rock group Midnight Oil surprised the organizers by unveiling clothing simply emblazoned with the word 'Sorry'. The reaction from the crowd of more than 100,000 was rapturous.

Importantly, and disappointingly, the Australian federal administration has failed to follow the lead of the people. Prime Minister John Howard has, on behalf of

The above photograph shows a typical native title meeting, where traditional owners negotiate with lawyers and anthropologists to establish the 'continuous occupation' required under the terms of the Native Title Act in the obvious absence of title deeds. This continuous occupation is complicated by people having been moved off their land at different points in history. In the hearings, knowledge and testimony to do with sacred sites and cultural traditions is tabled and a case is then presented to the courts.

his government, repeatedly refused to apologize to Indigenous Australians for the sufferings they have endured since the invasion. At the same time, there is no acknowledgment at the national level of the original inhabitants' prior ownership of Australia. Similarly, there is a refusal to honour the dead in the foundational battles (which themselves remain unrecognized), let alone to investigate the drafting of an appropriate treaty with the First Australians. For Australia, these remain some of the great unresolved issues of the new millennium.

The cultural renaissance

Ironically, while there has been a refusal to act in some areas, over the same period of time there has been considerable support for burgeoning Aboriginal achievements in the arts and cultural industries.

These considerable artistic and cultural achievements – in such areas as literature, film, photography, drama, dance, music and visual art – are in turn often highly politicized in support of Aboriginal rights, especially when such manifestations are being performed or presented overseas. This Indigenous artistic renaissance since the 1970s has been supported in part by the federal government, but more important has been the expression by a set of Indigenous communities of their ongoing political struggle.

In their own right, Aboriginal and Torres Strait Islander artists have had an incredible international impact over the past four decades. If there is any area that has defined the renaissance of Australian Indigenous culture globally, it is visual art. Yet it was only in the late 1950s that the collecting of Aboriginal bark paintings began in any serious way, and until the 1960s, that process was mainly confined to ethnographic museums, to the category of so-called 'primitive art' and to the generic category of 'art and craft' rather than to 'fine art'.

The past thirty years has seen a revolution in this field. Far from being a particular passion of anthropologists, Aboriginal art is now widely collected in the galleries of the world and is commonly sold through international art auction houses. In financial terms, Australian Indigenous art is, today, an industry worth more than

Above, a hundred thousand people converge in the parklands of the city of Melbourne to demand an official apology and a treaty with Indigenous Australia. Below right, Cathy Freeman, gold medallist in the 400 metres at the 2000 Sydney Olympics, proudly wearing the Aboriginal and Australian flags.

US$50 million per annum. In symbolic terms, the worth of such art to Australia is incalculable: it is a major attraction for international tourists, it is typically displayed with pride in every Australian diplomatic mission, and it regularly forms the backbone of touring exhibitions throughout the Northern hemisphere.

Whether it is Central Desert acrylic art, batik, contemporary urban painting, sculpture or traditional bark painting, Aboriginal art is a flagship for Australian Indigenous (and, arguably, for non-Indigenous) culture. It is an unparalleled example of the simultaneous influence of the intensely local and the international; those works that speak – at one and the same time – in a special land- and religion-centred way and are globally migratory. The key difference is that in this case both the local inspiration and the international impact emanate from Australian soil.

The 'Dreamings' exhibition that toured the US in 1988–89 had a major impact. More recently, 'The Native Born' toured in 2002 to three galleries in three different continents: the Palacio de Velázquez in Madrid, the Pinacoteca do Estado de São Paulo in Brazil and the Asia Society Museum in New York City. As exhibition curator Djon Mundine has put it, the paintings are far more than ochre and bark; they are 'an encyclopedia of the environment; a place, a site, a season, a being, a song, a dance, a ritual, an ancestral story and a personal history'.

Visual art has done much to render Indigenous culture more accessible to non-Aboriginal Australians and the international market alike. It has also been appropriated in effective ways by the corporate sector. The ultimate example of this commercial transformation was the creation by Qantas Airways, in collaboration with the Indigenous design house Balarinji, of what are claimed to be the 'largest flying artworks in the world'. The 1995 unveiling of the first jumbo jet adorned with Indigenous motifs from the central desert, dubbed 'Wunala Dreaming', was hugely successful and became one of the most-reported events in recent aviation history. Today, there are three Qantas aircraft painted in the livery of Aboriginal Australia. They have flown all over the globe, reinforcing the message that Australia's indigeneity is an extremely powerful travelling symbol for the nation.

The work of Aboriginal and Torres Strait Islander peoples is now highly visible while, at the same time, the artists themselves are relatively unknown and invisible. With some noteworthy exceptions – such as the work of Rover Thomas and Trevor Nickolls (both of whose paintings were

This Fire Dreaming *Warlu Jukurrpa*, (below) is passed on through the generations by the Nampitjinpa skin group in central Australia, which is why a group of women, Nampitjinpa sisters, are responsible for this Dreaming, and have the exclusive right to reproduce it in paint. The concentric circles represent the fires while the U-shapes are people in the story. The emu, who represents another skin group, is depicted by his footprints (the arrow shapes, backwards), walking the country. The dots represent sand dunes and areas of vegetation where the smoke and flames spread. Dots create a shimmering effect highly valued in Aboriginal art.

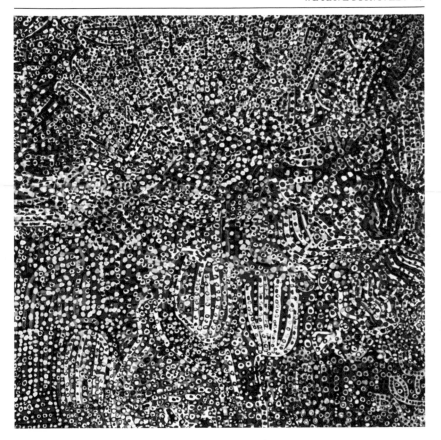

exhibited at the Venice Biennale of 1990) – Indigenous visual art is often far less personalized than that of the Euro-Australian tradition. However, there has also been an inexorable trend towards the identification of a canon of outstanding Aboriginal artists, including the painters Emily Kame Kngwarreye and Clifford Possum Tjapaltjarri, the sculptor and mixed-media artist Lin Onus and the photographer and film-maker Tracey Moffatt.

Literature

Today, Indigenous artists are in the Australian public eye more than ever before; the field of literature is one of the

Emily Kame Kngwarreye started painting at the Utopia community in south Central Australia at the age of 70. Painting with acrylics on canvas, she worked fast, abstracting traditional motifs with a dot or line technique. *Untitled* (above) is an early painting from her sought-after and highly valued oeuvre.

This *Water Dreaming*, painted in 1971 by Old Walter Tjampitjinpa (left) is a modern version of a traditional set of icons: the wavy lines represent the Rainbow Serpent, and the concentric circle is a water hole. The previous pages show a work by Tim Leurah Tjapaltjarri, one of the finest of the Papunya painters, who here, at a very early stage of the school in 1971, was beginning to add more of a bright acrylic palette to the traditional ochre tones. Since the time when teacher Geoffrey Bardon helped introduce the movement to canvas, Papunya art has evolved a good deal, as is shown in this painting by Mick Namarari Tjapaltjarri (opposite), produced in 1980. Here he is pushing to the limit the symbolism of the parallel line. Papunya art styles opened the door for many other communities of artists, at Kintore, Yuendumu, Lajamanu, Utopia and Balgo Hills, giving rise to a national art movement. Today most Aboriginal communities have art co-operatives run by agents who manage materials, sales and commissions.

most significant in this regard. For example, in 1999 novelist Kim Scott was the first Indigenous Australian to win the coveted Miles Franklin Award, with his novel *Benang*. This followed the successes of scores of Black Australian poets, playwrights, authors of fiction, life stories and autobiographies by such artists as Oodgeroo, Kevin Gilbert, Jack Davis, Mudrooroo, Archie Weller, Melissa Lucashenko, Alexis Wright, Sally Morgan, Jackie Huggins, Doris Pilkington, Roger Harding, Jared Thomas and Vivienne Cleven. Of these, Morgan is one of the best-known internationally by virtue of her best-selling life story, *My Place*, which had sold well in excess of 500,000 copies worldwide by 2004. However, a cross-over from fiction to film has seen Pilkington's *Travel the Rabbit-Proof Fence* become one of the most significant feature films inspired by an Indigenous story.

Film, drama, television

Crossing boundaries is a hallmark of contemporary Indigenous achievement. The accomplished Aboriginal actor Deborah Mailman (who was the first Indigenous Australian to win an Australian Film Institute Best Actress Award for her role in the 1997 film *Radiance*, directed by Rachel Perkins) is also a successful stage and television performer. She has appeared in shows as varied as Shakespeare's *Taming of the Shrew* and the top-rating television series *The Secret Life of Us*, and she is the co-author of the acclaimed one-woman drama, *The 7 Stages of Grieving*, which she co-wrote with director Wesley Enoch. Mailman is a highly influential performer with a strong commitment to the practical and the political. As she says: 'I would always encourage Indigenous actors to train... acting gives me the opportunity to change perception, create debate, educate people and tell my story... I intend to be around for a long time.'

Comedian and actor Ernie Dingo is one of the most recognized Indigenous faces on Australian television, as is actor Aaron Pedersen. In popular music, performers such as Archie Roach, Ruby Hunter and Christine Anu, as well as groups like Yothu Yindi (with lead singer Mandawuy Yunupingu), Tiddas and Coloured Stone have helped to define a distinctive genre of Indigenous

This huge canvas (8 by 10 metres) represents an 80,000-hectare area of the Great Sandy Desert and was executed collectively by 70 artists from the Mangala, Walmajarri, Wangkajungka and Juwaliny language groups. It was submitted as evidence of affiliation with the land at a Native Title plenary conference in June 1997 that negotiated between the native title claimants, the Western Australian State Government and other non-Aboriginal interest groups.

Australian music. Meanwhile, singer-performers like Leah Purcell and Rosie Ningali-Lawford have re-cast the one-woman show in entirely new ways and opera singer Maroochy Barambah made a significant mark throughout the period. No matter what field of the arts, whether it is sculpture, stilt-walking or song-poetry, Aboriginal and Islander artists have had a major impact.

One showcase of the sea-change in this area was the first of the pre-Olympic Arts Festivals, held in Sydney in 1997. With Indigenous artistic director Rhoda Roberts at the helm, the Festival of the Dreaming was probably the most influential Indigenous arts festival ever held in Australia. Over two weeks it featured in excess of 100 performances from all over the country as well as from many other First Nations globally. It emphasized the incredible diversity, and talent, of Aboriginal and Torres Strait Islander cultures.

The Ngurrara Native Title Claim covers much of the Great Sandy Desert, where some people, who had hardly even seen Europeans, came out of the desert only three decades ago. Yet the claim process still demands proof of traditional association, illustrated above in a spectacular fashion as a dancer performs his 'association'.

The centrality of Indigenous Australia

So what does all this achievement signify? Clearly, Australian culture cannot now be thought of without placing Aboriginal and Torres Strait Island cultures at its core. But, if it is recognized as integral to Australia's self-definition, why is it that so many Indigenous Australians live in marginal conditions akin to those of developing nations? The starkly different values attributed to Aboriginality are a sign of the cultural and economic dilemmas of these communities at the end of empire.

One response is that governmental promotion of those appealing (and commercially viable) aspects of Aboriginality may divert attention away from the far more difficult problems of domestic violence, substance abuse, and deaths in custody. A graphic reminder of this continuity of conflict occurred in February 2004, when the Indigenous community in the suburb of Redfern in Sydney erupted after the death of a seventeen-year-old Aboriginal youth, Thomas James Hickey. Sadly, in one sense, it can be argued that little has changed since the days of Governor Phillip and Bennelong.

Aden Ridgeway (above left), a Gumbayynggirr man from New South Wales, has been using his position as a Federal Senator for the Australian Democrats to push reconciliation issues. Jared Thomas (above right), from Port Augusta in South Australia, is a younger Indigenous writer. His play *Flash Red Ford* has also been staged in Kenya and Uganda, countries where Indigenous concerns are also highlighted.

But, in another sense that is untrue. For it is undoubtedly the case that today the issue of agency and of motivation is vastly different. Indigenous Australians now choose and aspire to varied careers, seek to express their own culture and distinctiveness on canvas, on stage, on dance floors, computer screens and film sets. And it is equally the case that the achievements of Aboriginal performers and artists do inspire all Indigenous Australians – both politically and practically – just as the contributions of Aboriginal doctors, teachers and magistrates act as catalysts for other First Australians to pursue education in these areas.

At its heart, this signifies a remarkable achievement. Aboriginal and Torres Strait Islander people have, despite everything that has occurred in the past, not only survived but have excelled, in so many ways, both internationally and domestically. They have always been members of powerful communities: they have maintained their cultural integrity from the beginnings of imperial invasion to 'the end of Empire' in the present day. The next decade may just see full recognition of that past and that Indigenous future.

Rhoda Roberts (above left), of Bundjalung origins, is an author, actor and director. She has been a leading actor in television since the 1990s. In 1997 she took on the task of directing the biggest festival of Indigenous arts ever held, the Festival of the Dreaming. Patrick Johnson (above right) is of Umpila origin in the Gulf country. An Olympic Games contender since 1998, he is now the fastest man in Australia, running 100 metres in under 10 seconds.

Overleaf, *Jailhouse Creek* by renowned Indigenous artist Rover Thomas.

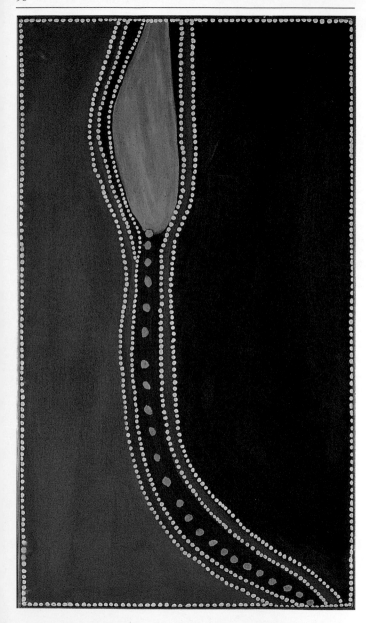

DOCUMENTS

Ethnographic viewpoints

As figures like Durkheim (sociology) and Freud (psychoanalysis) were developing their modern human sciences in Europe, they saw in the Indigenous Australians a primitive counterpoint, a rich resource for what humans were like at some basic level. Influenced by a long line of evolutionist and functionalist thinking, it would be some time before they could see Indigenous Australians as existing at the same time as them, even as they recognized the complexity of Aboriginal civilization.

Every man has a totem

Sigmund Freud was intrigued by the concept of totemism, the belief which held that humans could have an intimate kinship with plants and animals. In his celebrated essay of 1913, 'Totem and Taboo', he analyses this phenomenon and its psychoanalytic significance with several peoples: the Masai of East Africa, certain Arabic peoples, and the Australian Aborigines. His comments on the social practices of the first Australians and his psychonalysis of the spiritual significance of totemism remain pertinent.

The aborigines of Australia are looked upon as a peculiar race which shows neither physical nor linguistic relationship with its nearest neighbours, the Melanesian, Polynesian and Malayan races. They do not build houses or permanent huts; they do not cultivate the soil or keep any domestic animals except dogs; and they do not even know the art of pottery. They live exclusively on the flesh of all sorts of animals which they kill in the chase, and on the roots which they dig. Kings or chieftains are unknown among them, and all communal affairs are decided by the elders in assembly. It is quite doubtful whether they evince any traces of religion in the form of the worship of higher beings. The tribes living in the interior who have to contend with the greatest vicissitudes of life owing to a scarcity of water, seem in every way more primitive than those who live near the coast.

...Australian tribes are divided into smaller septs or clans, each taking the name of its totem. Now what is a totem? As a rule it is an animal, either edible and harmless, or dangerous and feared; more rarely the totem is a plant or a force of nature (rain, water), which stands in a peculiar relation to the whole clan. The totem is first of all the tribal ancestor of the clan, as well as its tutelary spirit and protector; it sends oracles and, though otherwise dangerous, the totem knows and spares its children. The members of a totem are therefore under a sacred obligation not to kill (destroy) their totem, to abstain from eating its meat or from any other which members of a totem represent or imitate, in ceremonial dances, the movements and characteristics of their totems.

The totem is hereditary either through the maternal or paternal line; (maternal transmission probably always preceded and was only later supplanted by the paternal). The attachment to a totem is the foundation of all the social obligations of an Australian: it extends on the one hand beyond the tribal relationship, and on the other hand it supersedes consanguineous relationship.

The totem is not limited to district or to locality; the members of a totem may live separated from one another and on friendly terms with adherents of other totems.

Sigmund Freud, *Totem and Taboo: Resemblances between the Psychic Lives of Savages and Neurotics*, trans. A. A. Brill, Routledge, London, 1919, pp. 2–4

Two ethnographers in the field

In 1894 Baldwin Spencer (1860–1929), Professor of Biology and aesthete and Francis Gillen (1855–1912), postmaster at the telegraph station in Alice Springs in the heart of Australia, decided to collaborate on a study of the Arrernte tribe. In 1899 they published The Native Tribes of Central Australia, *and later various other works, including photography, which became classics in the field and sources for the more 'armchair' pursuits of Europeans like the Scottish mythologist J. G. Frazer, the French sociologist Emile Durkheim and the Austrian Sigmund Freud. Spencer and Gillen's documentation was extensive and their understanding profound.*

At the end of the 19th century white photographers tended to take studio shots of Indigenous Australians; many of these were published as postcards.

enjoyment of it. Any violation of these prohibitions is automatically punished. The character of a totem is inherent not only in a single animal or a single being but in all the members of the species. From time to time, festivals are held at

From time immemorial – that is, as far back as ever native traditions go – the boundaries of the tribes have been where they are now fixed. Within them their ancestors roamed about, hunting and performing their ceremonies just as their living descendants do at the present day. There has never apparently been the least attempt made by one tribe to encroach upon the territory of another. ...No idea of this or of its advisability or otherwise ever enters the head of the Central Australian native. Very probably this is to be associated with the fundamental belief that his *alcheringa* ancestors occupied precisely the same country which he does now. The spirit parts of these ancestors are still there, and he has a vague kind of an idea not only that the country is indubitably his by right of inheritance, but that it would be of no use to any one else, nor would any other people's country be good for him. The spirit individuals would not permanently leave their old home, and where they are there must he stay.

W. Baldwin Spencer and F. J. Gillen, *The Northern Tribes of Central Australia*, Macmillan, London, 1904, pp. 13–14

New perspectives

From the 1950s the fieldwork of A. P. Elkin started to provide the empirical basis for the correction of the Freudian interpretation of totemism and the perception of evolution from primitivity. This former Anglican priest became one of the major world figures of Anthropology, and his work on Aborigines is a valuable resource. He was the founder of a protectionist philanthropic association and of the prestigious journal Oceania *which he edited until his death in 1979. Elkin occupied the paradoxical position of respecting the Aboriginal cultures with which he had passed years in the field in the Kimberley and the Northern Territory,*

and yet believing that assimilation was the only viable policy for their future. In the following passage he reflects on the place of women in Indigenous society.

Although women are not admitted to the 'inner sanctuary' of sacred rituals, yet, as we have known for many years, they do play a subsidiary role in most of them. They are in the 'nave', and sometimes even in the 'chancel'. Their part varies in different regions and according to the ceremonies. For example, with regard to men's initiation, the women play quite a conspicuous part in the tooth-avulsion and pre-circumcision dances in south Kimberley, but are nowhere near the scene of circumcision and do not see the initiand again until his formal return to the camp after recovery. In southern Arnhem Land, however, while the women only dance inconspicuously during the pre-circumcision dances, a number of 'sisters' are present at the actual operation, processing around the mass of men who completely hide the candidate. Indeed, I have seen women relatives bringing the initiand along behind the Songman to the place of the operation on the edge of the camp.

The secret life proper comes after initiation, and into that women are nowhere admitted in the same way and in the same degree as the men are. On the other hand they do possess cult totems, or 'dreamings', as these are called, so that they are potential or threshold members of cult-lodges and the secret life. Their brothers, or whoever are the male members of their cult-society, perform the ceremonies for them. According to the myths of some tribes, women originally owned the ceremonies, but let the men take them and henceforth act on their behalf. They

Kimberley Aborigines, photographed by the ethnographer A. P. Elkin in the 1950s.

are also credited with introducing the stone circumcision knife in some regions, to replace the crude fire-stick 'surgical instrument' which the men had been using. In the north-west of the continent they take a direct part in some rituals of increase for natural species which they gather.

To sum up: Women play a part in all important sacred rituals. It may consist of observing prescribed taboos while the men are in the secret places; chanting; answering ritual calls; being present as observers or as minor participants in final scenes just off the secret ground or at the general camp; and preparing food. The older women know the sequence of rites as well as their own roles, and direct the younger women in their duties and observances. One or two old women may hold officially authority over the rest, although an old man is usually left in the camp to see that all rules are kept.

We can therefore speak of sacred ritual proceeding simultaneously at two levels: the men's secret level; and the camp level, the province of the women. The levels are for the most part on parallel planes, but they meet from time to time. This occurs more often in the tropical north than in the arid interior. In the Maraian ceremonies of Arnhem Land, for example, the men return every afternoon to the camp where, still bearing on their bodies their painted ritual designs, they dance around two ceremonial forked poles or 'trees'. The women meet them, and not only dance in the background, but also join with them in some scenes.

A. P. Elkin, *The Australian Aborigines*, Angus & Robertson, Sydney, 1974, 5th fully rev. ed., pp. 213–214

Religion and power

One of the great interpreters of Australian Indigenous cultures, W. E. H. Stanner, shows his awareness (in the passage below) of the power and significance of the sacred sites, and the difficulty of translating this power and meaning. The passage also demonstrates the ethic of sharing knowledge; from black to white, from older person to younger.

Scholars familiar with Aborigines have usually had one impressive experience in common: to be taken by Aboriginal friends to places in the wilds and there shown something – tree, rocky outcrop, cranny, pool – with formality, pride and love. Conversations follow rather like this: 'There is my Dreaming [place]. My father showed me this place when I was a little boy. His father showed him.' Perhaps a child stands near by, all eyes and ears. Here is a tradition being made continuous, as in the past, by overlapping life-spans. What had his father said? 'He said: "Your Dreaming is there; you want to look after this place; you don't want to let it go [forget, be careless about it]; it is from the first [totemical] man."' The historical link is thus made: from the now old to the still young; from the living to the anciently dead; from the very first true man to next true man; from the oldest time to the here and now. (Down with a crash come the needless postulates of racial and collective unconscious.) What did the father do there? 'He used to come here every year with the old men, the wise men; they used to do something here [hit, rub, break off pieces, brush with green leaves, sing]; that way they made the [totem] come on, come back, jump up, spread out.' How did that happen? What is it that is in the place?

'We do not know. Something is there. Like my spirit [soul, shadow, invisible counterpart]; like my Dreaming [naming the totem entity].' Will he think more? What else did his father say? That there was something in the Dreaming-place? The dark eyes turn and look intent, puzzled, searching. 'My father did not say. He said this: "My boy, look! Your Dreaming is there; it is a big thing; you never let it go [pass it by]; all Dreamings [totem entities] come from there; your spirit is there."' Does the white man now understand? The blackfellow, earnest, friendly, makes a last effort. 'Old man, you listen! Something is there; we do not know what; something.' There is a struggle to find words, and perhaps a lapse into English. 'Like engine, like power, plenty of power, it does hard work; it pushes.'

W. E. H. Stanner, 'Religion, Totemism and Symbolism', in R. M. Berndt and C. H. Berndt, *Aboriginal Man in Australia*, Angus & Robertson, Sydney, 1965

'Women's business'

In 1983, the Australian feminist ethnographer Diane Bell published a work called Daughters of the Dreaming, *which represented a break from an anthropology that was hitherto largely masculinist. She was one of the first, together with Catherine Berndt and Nancy Munn, to reveal much about the importance of gendered aspects of women's cultural life, which was often not made available to male researchers: their specific sites, their sacred 'business', their songs and rituals.*

In Aboriginal society both men and women base their claims to status within their society on their direct access to the *jukurrpa*, but each then elaborates their rights and responsibilities within separate domains. An understanding of sexual politics therefore must be based on knowledge of the power base of each sex and the way in which male and female domains are connected. A corollary to this argument is that the separation of the sexes does not solve the tensions engendered by male–female relations: it merely orders certain aspects of the sets of relationships within and between the domains of men and women. Our understanding of sexual politics within Aboriginal society is skewed because we have inadequately explored the nature of women's power base. By setting up a framework for understanding women's rituals which relates the tensions of sexual politics to the far-reaching impact of recent social and cultural changes, I have depicted the relation between the sexes as an ever-shifting, negotiable balance. Women's rituals then become both an element in the balance and an indication of the state of the balance.

In ritual the Law is made known in a highly stylized and emotionally charged manner: the separation of the sexes, so evident in daily activities, reaches its zenith. Ritual may therefore be considered as an important barometer of male-female relations, for it provides, as it were, an arena in which the values of the society are writ large, where the sex division of labour is starkly drawn and explored by the participants. It was in ritual that I found men and women clearly stating their own perceptions of their role, their relationship to the opposite sex and their relation to the Dreamtime whence all legitimate authority and power once flowed. However, while women and men today, as in the past, maintain separate spheres of interaction, the evaluations of their respective roles and their opportunities to achieve status have fundamentally altered during a century of white intrusion into Central Australia. Men and women have been differently affected in the shift from a hunter-gatherer mode of subsistence to a sedentary life-style on large institutionalized government settlements.

Within the historical context of Aboriginal society, the maintenance of male–female relations entailed a continuing dialogue which allowed women to participate actively in the construction of the cultural evaluations of their role in their society. But today, as members of a colonial frontier society, Aboriginal women no longer participate as equals in this process. Women's solidarity and autonomy are being eroded and devalued. They are constrained and defined by the male-dominated frontier society as a necessarily dependent sex. The inter-relations between the sexes are thus no longer shaped predominantly by the set of male–female relations of Aboriginal society; the new forces of the wider colonial society affect them too. The activities of men and women within this new order are differently evaluated and different opportunities for participation are available to men and women.

Diane Bell, *Daughters of the Dreaming*, Spinifex Press, North Melbourne, 2002, 3rd ed.

The language of the Dreaming

For a long time Aboriginal plastic arts were tied to specific places, bodies and ceremonies and were not produced for sale or exhibition. In the 1970s, people were encouraged to produce paintings on bark or canvas, and a new chapter began in the history of Australian art as an authentic and ancient set of images reasserted itself over the more ephemeral art forms of the settlers. Far from being fixed, these images were original and modern, yet continuously reaching back to the Dreaming cultures for inspiration.

A European discovers Aboriginal art

Between 1956 and 1960, Karel Kupka, a Czech-born painter, made three trips to Northern Australia where he collected a large number of bark paintings. In 1962 he published Dawn of Art, *the first book to show to Europe 'the unique cultural expression which [he] had the good fortune to encounter'. This was followed up with other publications and gifts of artworks to museums. His was an early and genuine artistic interest that helped draw Aboriginal art out of the narrow domain of the ethnographic artefact.*

Art is constantly present in the life of the Aborigines. Apart from the sacred objects used in ancestral rites, they paint, engrave, or carve their weapons and tools and everyday implements. Rocks, bark shelters, and even the ground itself are often decorated with paintings; ornamental patterns are drawn in the sand, and many trees were embellished with carving. The majestic sculptural mortuary poles and the hollow logs destined to house the bones of the dead are richly painted, as are the corpses and, after the flesh has decomposed, the skulls. The bones are painted with red ochre, as were those of some prehistoric men of hunting cultures that have been dug out of their resting places by archaeologists. These ritual and artistic activities have survived down to our own day in all their traditional purity, but they are now followed less and less frequently. Modern civilization opens too many prospects to the more recent generations of Aborigines and tends to diminish their interest in ancestral customs. However, European culture has had only superficial influences on their culture, which can be explained by the lack of common denominators between the two. The gap is too great for convergence to be possible. The transformation of the Aborigines' way of life does indeed condemn their arts to extinction, but for as long as the old traditions survive they will keep their essential characteristics. Comparison of

Karel Kupka in 1956, on the occasion of his visit to the exhibition of Aboriginal Art at the East Sydney Technical College.

the most ancient and the most recent work, whether rock-wall paintings or rock engraving, shows the continuity that distinguishes Aboriginal plastic arts.

While a surprising unity of conception can be found in the arts of the Australian Aborigines, considerable differences in form occur from one region to another. These differences appear most strikingly in the case of painting. Perhaps natural conditions favoured the development of one form of art rather than another in Australia, just as in other continents.

Karel Kupka, *Dawn of Art: Painting and Sculpture of Australian Aborigines*, Angus & Robertson, Sydney, 1965, pp. 53–54

Shade and memory

Art is sensual and full of power and meaning which comes from its status as event achieved in ritual or ceremony. Songs and dances accompanying the visual allow the participants to impregnate their bodies with the story of the ancestor. Time knots and binds in a ritual during which the images are traced, then erased as the ceremony finishes and the power returns to the earth.

What then is Aboriginal visual art? It is an expression of Aboriginal philosophy in form and colour and in design which has an aspect of beauty according to the tradition of the tribes concerned. It is not primarily an attempt to produce the beautiful for its own sake, though it does reveal aesthetic appreciation. Aboriginal art is first and foremost a ritual activity, correlated with chanting, dancing and acting – the other components in most rites. Chanting over the 'pretty' patterns of a secret bull-roarer in the Flinders Range of South Australia; greasing and devotionally rubbing the grooves of the designs on Central Australian *tjurunga*: chanting while the actors are being painted to 'become' the Dreaming heroes in the western desert of South Australia, or while the initiated are being painted to participate in a clan's 'dreaming' in Arnhem Land; painting and retouching the Wondjina cave paintings of North Kimberley to make their Dreaming power effective again; painting mythological designs on bark, emblems and carved human figures to bring the 'dreaming' present: these are expressions of the belief that by re-presenting the 'dreaming' or creative heroic past which is still present though unseen, the tribes and natural species are again brought within the effective influence of that creative past. The painting is the visible sign and sacrament of the 'dreaming', just as the chanting is its audible sign, and the acting by the painted and transformed actors is its dramatic form.

Man and all that is has two aspects: the material which is seen, and the 'shade' or soul which is not seen – at least usually. Neither can be ignored. The heritage of knowledge of the environment and of skills deals with the one; the heritage of art and ritual channels the other. This latter is the ordered arrangement of symbols, symbolic actions, designs and sounds, in an attempt to express in outward forms the 'shade', the inner life and meaning, the permanent element, in man and the world in the present, past and future.

Here, too, lies the significance of designs on weapons, implements and ornaments. It comes as a surprise to see on these objects the same designs engraved or painted, which are associated with sacred symbols and emblems, and treated so reverentially on secret ritual occasions. The point, however, of secret ritual, which is performed as it were in the world of the 'shade', is to make the unseen effective and active in the everyday world. Therefore, these designs often come forth from the sacred life of mythology, of doctrine and belief, from the 'world of the shades', and so provide for the 'shade', for the unseen and contingent element in the use of those everyday objects which bear their mark.

A. P. Elkin, *The Australian Aborigines*, Angus & Robertson, Sydney, 1974, 5th fully rev. ed., pp. 278–279

Papunya Tula painting

In 1971, at Papunya in the Western desert, a teacher named Geoffrey Bardon encouraged elders to render their Dreamings on the walls of the school house. Thus was born a new school of painting which spread to other centres. A thousand paintings were produced in a year, and exhibitions and catalogues assured the reception of the work from New York to Paris. This artistic movement has no rival in contemporary Australia. Here, curators Hetti Perkins and Hannah Fink explain its traditional origins.

Generally speaking, and on their most literal level, the paintings are maps, charting the cast terrain of the Western Desert and its minutest detail — from the travels of the Tingari to the tiny scratchings in the sand of a bandicoot. The notion of movement or momentum is intrinsic to indigenous desert life. The artists themselves travel widely, as did their ancestors, and the stories they depict primarily concern the creative journeys of ancestral men, women and supernatural beings.

The contemporary visions of today's artists spring from this ancient tradition. Land in Papunya Tula painting is corporeal and this familial relationship to country is quintessentially expressed by symbols painted on the body. Since the early 1970s, this connection has been amplified through the introduced media of acrylic and canvas, a contemporary elaboration of the ochres and plant matter of the ephemeral ground paintings used in ceremony. The method of creating the paintings, involving the execution of a design on a plain ground and then infilling sections with dense or sparsely applied points of colour, emulates the labour-intensive construction of low relief sandpaintings in which an often vast section of flattened, ochred earth, decorated with ancestral designs, is embellished with white flecks of wamulu.

Hetti Perkins and Hannah Fink, 'Genesis and Genius: The Art of Papunya Tula Artists', in *Papunya Tula: Genesis and Genius*, Art Gallery of New South Wales, Sydney, 2000, p. 174

The tradition of desert painting

Vast regions of the central and western parts of the Australian continent, including much of the Northern Territory, South Australia and Western Australia, are covered by geographical deserts, a word which implies harsh and barren landscapes. The Australian deserts appear empty and inhospitable to those who do not know them, but to the Aboriginal groups who inhabit these areas, the lands created by their ancestors and infused with their powers are places rich in spiritual meaning and physical sustenance.

The deserts are also the home of one of the most important movements in contemporary Australian art, for, while artists continue the traditional practice of painting on the ground, on their material possessions such as shields, wooden dishes and boomerangs, and on their bodies, they now use acrylic paint and canvases to carry the classical idioms of desert art to a wider audience than was previously possible.

Geographically, the desert includes mountain ranges and spectacular rock formations, grassy plains, stands of eucalypt and mulga trees, lakes, salt pans, sandhills, and stretches of stony country occasionally broken by seasonal watercourses and rivers and punctuated by rare permanent rockholes, springs, waterholes and soakages. The region is home to a number of Aboriginal groups who in the main share common cosmology and social systems, as well as common art traditions, and who form a major cultural bloc in Aboriginal Australia. Across this landscape spreads a web of ancestral paths travelled by the supernatural beings on their epic journeys of creation in the *Jukurrpa* or Dreaming, linking the topography firmly to the social order of the people.

The impact of European incursions and settlement on the peoples of the Australian desert was different from that on Arnhem Land. The first European explorers entered central Australia in 1860, and by 1885 much of the best grazing land around present-day Hermannsburg was occupied by pastoralists. Cattle and sheep polluted waterholes, and the new land-holders forced many groups of Aboriginal people away from their traditional lands. Other adverse consequences of European settlement, such as the spread of new diseases and the influx of refugees from the newly settled areas, had an impact on Aboriginal groups right across the desert, in some cases nearly a century before they sighted Europeans for the first time. Nevertheless, Aboriginal people were able to continue their relationships to their lands despite the wholesale takeovers by working on the pastoral stations, and by ensuring the continuity of rich oral traditions and ceremonies through which the land was celebrated and vivified.

The physical dislocation accelerated in the twentieth century as settlement spread. In 1941 Haasts Bluff, west of Alice Springs, was declared a reserve, and by 1955 Government settlements were established at Yuendumu and Lajamanu, with the last settlement of the assimilation era created at Papunya in 1960. Until 1966, under Government policies Aboriginal people were taken to live in these settlements, bringing them together in the most inappropriate social circumstances with detrimental effects on their cultural practices.

Federal political changes of the 1970s permitted and even encouraged people to return to live on their ancestral lands. Today, the desert towns of Papunya, Yuendumu, Lajamanu and others service many often distant outstations that have sprung up since 1970. The Aboriginal councils in these towns have established cooperatives to cater for artists' needs, and to channel art from the outlying areas to the galleries of the cities. The cooperatives operate as buffers between the traditional social and cultural concerns of the artists and the demands and expectations of the outside world.

Classical desert art takes many forms, from decorated weapons and implements to personal adornments, from sacred and secret incised boards and stones, often called *tjuringa*, to rock engravings and paintings, and the more ephemeral arts of body painting, sand drawings, ceremonial constructions and ground paintings. While the classical traditions continue, the introduced media such as acrylic paint and canvas are usually employed for the purposes of public art.

Recently introduced techniques of dating rock engravings, and the persistence of similar painted images recorded in the nineteenth century, reveal that designs that are commonly in use today for both ceremonial and public paintings have been continuously produced in the desert for many millennia.

The basic elements of the pictorial art are limited in number but broad in meaning. The iconography of desert art is a language separate and distinct from that of Arnhem Land. Characteristic of the range of conventional designs and icons are those denoting place or site, and those indicating paths or movement. Concentric circles may denote a site, a camp, a waterhole or a fire. In ceremony, the concentric circle provides the means for the ancestral power which lies within the earth to surface and go back into the ground. Meandering and straight lines may indicate lightning or water courses, or they may describe the paths of ancestors and supernatural beings. Tracks of animals and humans are also part of the lexicon of desert imagery. U-shapes usually represent settled people or breasts, while arcs may be boomerangs or wind-breaks, and short straight lines or bars are often spears and digging sticks. Fields of dots can indicate sparks, fire, burnt ground, smoke, clouds, rain, and other phenomena.

The interpretations of these designs are multiple and simultaneous, and depend upon the viewer's ritual knowledge of a site and the associated Dreaming. The meanings are elaborated and enhanced by the various combinations or juxtapositions of designs in the paintings, and also by the social and cultural contexts within which they operate – whether for ceremony or the public domain, for instance. The combinations of designs allow an endless depth of meaning, and artists in describing their work distinguish between those meanings which are intended for public revelation and those which are not, and provide the appropriate level of interpretation.

Wally Caruana, *Aboriginal Art*, Thames & Hudson, London and New York, 2nd edition, 2003, pp. 101–103

Petitioning and persuading

Most early writing by Indigenous peoples took the form of petitions or short journalism, and it dated from the 1830s, with the publication in Tasmania of the Flinders Island Chronicle. *Ever since there has been a constant stream of interventions in the press and other media in which Indigenous people have put their case as forcefully as possible.*

Where do my people come from?

A Ngarrindjeri man from South Australia, David Unaipon (1872–1967) was among the first Indigenous writers to be published. As well as writing articles, poems and stories, he was also an acclaimed public speaker and a skilled inventor and engineer. The Australian $50 note commemorates his achievements.

… Since coming to Australia thousands of years ago, there has been probably little or no change in the habits and customs of my people. They have kept the balance of Nature; for centuries they have neither advanced nor retrogressed.

Our tribal laws and customs are fixed and interchangeable. Generation after generation has gone through the same rigid tribal training.

Every race has had its great traditional leader and law-giver, who has given the race its first moral training as well as its social and tribal customs. Nar-ran-darrie was our great traditional leader. The laws of Nar-ran-darrie are taught to the children in their infancy. The hunting grounds were given out to the different families and tribes by Nar-ran-darrie. The boundaries of the tribal hunting grounds have been kept the same from remotest time. Whilst the children of the tribes are hearing from their elders all the traditions and legends of our race, they are learning all the knowledge and skills of bush craft and hunting, as well as undergoing the three great tests or initiations to 'kornmund' or full manhood and 'meemund', full womanhood, which is generally completed at the age of eighteen.

The first test is to overcome the appetite, by doing two days walk or hunt without food, and then to be brought suddenly before a fire, on which is cooking some choice kangaroo steak or other native delicacy.

The next test is to overcome pain. The young boys and girls submit to having their noses pierced, their bodies marked, and to lying down upon hot embers, thinly covered with boughs.

The third test is to overcome fear. The young people are told fearful and hair-raising stories about ghosts and the Mall-dar-pee, the evil spirit, or the devil-devil. After all this they are put to sleep in a lonely place or near the burial places of the tribe. During the night the elders, made hideous with white clay and bark headdresses, appear, making weird noises.

An Aboriginal camp, in a classic image collected by Nicolas Peterson of the ANU.

Those who can show no signs of having had a disturbed night are then admitted as fully initiated members of the tribe.

No youth or maiden is allowed to marry until he or she has passed these tests. The marriage is talked over first by all the old members of the tribe, and it is always the uncle of the young man who selects the wife. The uncle on the mother's side is the most important relative. The actual marriage takes place during the time of festivals.

The husband does not look or speak to his mother-in-law, although he is husband in name to all his sisters-in-law. Under native conditions the sex laws are very strict.

A fully developed Aboriginal has, in his own way, a vast amount of knowledge. Although it may not be strictly scientific learning, still it is a very exact knowledge, and his powers of physical observation are developed to the utmost. For instance, an Aboriginal, living under primitive life, knows the habits and the anatomy and the haunts of every animal in the bush. He knows all the birds, their habits, and even their love or mating notes. He knows the approach of different seasons of the year from various signs, as well as from the position of the stars in the heavens. He has developed the art of tracking the human footprint to the highest degree. There is a whole science in footprints. Footprints are the same evidence to a bush native as fingerprints are in a court of law.

He knows the track of every individual member of the tribe. There is as much difference and individuality in footprint as in fingerprints. Of course, it will be readily understood that the Aboriginal language and customs vary a great deal according to the nature of the country the tribes are living in. Although there is a great common understanding running through us all. Our legends and traditions are all the same tales, or myths, told slightly differently with local colouring, etc....

There is not the slightest hint in any of our traditions that there were any other previous inhabitants in Australia.

The greatest time of the year to my people is the 'Parr-barrarrie', the spring time. It is then that all the great traditional corroborees take place. All our sacred traditions are then chanted and told.

All the stars and constellations in the heavens, the Milky Way, the Southern Cross, Orion's Belt, the Magellan

Cloud, etc. have a meaning. There are legends connected with them all. We call the heavens the 'WY-erriewar' and the ruler of the heavens 'Nebalee'.

From time immemorial we have understood the art of hypnotic suggestion. Our medicine men, the 'Moon-cum-bulli' have used charms, etc. to drive out pain.

It will be seen from the foregoing account, and from other sources, that my race, living under tribal and native conditions, have a very strict and efficacious code of laws that keeps the race pure. It is only where the Aboriginal comes in contact with white civilisation that they leave their tribal laws, and take nothing in place of these old and well-established customs. It is then that disease and deterioration set in.

David Unaipon, 'Aboriginals. Their Traditions and Customs. Where Did They Come From?', *Daily Telegraph* (Sydney), Saturday 2 August 1924

'Still such a long way to go'

Pat O'Shane, born in 1941, was the first Aboriginal person to obtain a law degree. Minister of Aboriginal Affairs in New South Wales from 1982 to 1986, she has served as a magistrate for many years. Known for her bold public pronouncements, she says that 'the important thing is that I have proven to women and also to Aboriginal people more generally, that they are capable of doing what I have done.'

Twenty-five years ago, Aborigines were not counted in the first Australian Census. Animals, particularly livestock, were and thus the Australian government formalised the contemporary racist thinking that Aborigines were not only less than human, but less than animals. I grew up in North Queensland, where the then Native Protection Act defined the Aborigines and provided that they were subject to the Act. Although my grandfather had gained his exemption from the Act many years before, the fact that I was defined as Aboriginal brought me within the purview of its provisions, and I was always under threat of being taken from my family and placed on a reserve.

Therefore the prospect of a change to the Constitution such that the federal government would have responsibility for Aboriginal affairs and could make laws with respect to Aborigines was one that gave us considerable hope of substantial changes in relation to such legislation.

The campaign for the change to the Constitution was a long and difficult one. At the time, I was a member of the Aboriginal and Torres Strait Islander Advancement League, which was affiliated with the Federal Council for the Advancement of Aborigines and Torres Strait Islanders.

The FCAATSI decided about 1960 to campaign for the change, so this fight continued for almost seven years. I remember well the three years before the referendum (1967) when I, along with my mother and friends such as Joe McGuiness (FCAATSI President) and Jean Jimmy, addressed community meetings, trade unions, women's groups and church groups, and walked miles to distribute leaflets and talk to householders about the need for constitutional change.

At those meetings we received positive responses. Talking to individual householders was often a different experience. Dogs were set upon us, racist abuse screamed at us. The campaign had its ups and downs but in the event we were successful.

What we expected to flow from the constitutional change I'm not quite sure now – but certainly the mood was buoyant; expectant we would see an end to racist legislation and the implementation of human rights practices concerning Aborigines.

The 25 years since May 27, 1967 have been long and hard in bringing about those kind of changes. Nevertheless, change there has been. Certainly more Aborigines are employed today, while housing has also improved.

More Aboriginal children progress to university and into professional positions. But Australia cannot rest on its laurels – recent statistics show that the overall Aboriginal retention rate in education actually decreased between 1979 and 1990.

And as recently as 1990, the Department of Housing in NSW pointed out: 'Aboriginal need for rental accommodation is five times greater than that for the general population.' Australian Bureau of Statistics data from 1986 showed that the Aboriginal unemployment rate was four times that of non-Aborigines.

Further, it has been shown that Aborigines live on average 15–20 years less than other Australians, have infant mortality rates three times that of the rest of society and imprisonment rates up to eight times higher than non-Aborigines.

Those figures show that the quest for real citizenship – an equal share of society's rich resources – has a long way to go. With present proposals that the States take back responsibility for Aboriginal affairs, we might wonder at the real effects of the events of 1967.

Pat O'Shane, 'Still Such A Long Way To Go', *The Australian*, 27 May 1992

Ignorance of Aboriginal religion

Marcia Langton is Chair of the Australian Institute of Aboriginal and Torres Strait Islander Studies, and is Foundation Professor of Indigenous Studies at the University of Melbourne. An Indigenous person, she has been at the forefront of activist struggle and the collection and reorganization of Indigenous knowledge for the purposes of gaining land rights, policy change in government and eventually a treaty. Here she attacks the ignorance of Indigenous tradition that causes commentators to ridicule as 'secret women's business' the beliefs behind the attempt to block the construction of a bridge across the mouth of the Murray River in South Australia in 1995.

I do not know much about the facts of the Hindmarsh Bridge sacred sites case, and it is not proper that I should know.

However, I have worked on similar cases in parts of remote Australia for many years. I have observed that there are some consistent and structural similarities between this case and others in recent Australian history, which seem to have entirely escaped the notice of some of the cast in this drama.

All the basic elements of the current plot were present during the Coronation Hill inquiry by the Resources Assessment Commission. The Ancestor caught in that debate was Bula who lives in the Sickness Country near Coronation Hill.

The Jawoyn were labelled pagans, anti-Christians and anti-development by some. They, too, were accused of inventing sacred traditions. They stood their ground and gave evidence to the inquiry supported by expert opinion and documentation.

Today, the Jawoyn are joint venturers in aspects of other mining operations, have established a viable regional Aboriginal tourism plan, and aim for economic independence. They were awarded the inaugural Community of the Year Award by the National Australia Day Committee at New Year. Their economic success has depended on their ability to preserve and manage their cultural integrity. The protection of their sacred sites was a key feature of the Jawoyn saga.

Another event which unfolded similarly was the application by Arrente women in Alice Springs for the protection of women's sites under the Aboriginal Heritage Act in the face of a dam proposed by the Northern Territory Government.

After 15 years, several inquiries, an Australian Heritage Council listing, declaration of the sites by the then Sacred Sites Protection Authority of the NT, and many meetings and appeals by the women concerned, the Minister for Aboriginal Affairs, Mr Tickner, announced that he had issued an order preventing development of the area.

Likewise, these women who defended their religion and their sacred places were hounded and trivialised in the remote area media and by remote area politicians.

Eighteen years ago, the Ranger Uranium Environmental Inquiry (conducted by Justice Fox) into the proposed mine in the Alligator River region was surrounded by public debate and represented in the media in much the same way as the Hindmarsh Bridge affair has been presented.

The religious and mythical ancestors, particularly the Rainbow Serpent and Nagorrko, dangerous if provoked, were maligned by the proponents of 'progress', and Aboriginal people who sought protection of their lifestyle and of their religious life were pilloried as superstitious and backward. They were called 'stone age' on the front pages of several major newspapers.

Why is it so difficult for Aboriginal people to seek protection of places of great religious significance? Why do other Australians hold Aboriginal religion in such low esteem?

Aboriginal religion is being treated in the present public debate by ignorant people as if it were merely a superstitious and simple matter, easily dismissed and ridiculed. These people know nothing about Aboriginal religion and how it is transmitted, and they cannot know the facts of this case, nor the suffering they are causing to the members of the particular cult who are bravely defending a site of importance to women against destruction for a bridge and marina.

Calls for an inquiry into the beliefs of women in this case are a blatant attempt to promote and entrench religious intolerance that has too long marred the relationship between indigenous and non-indigenous Australians.

This is clearly election-mode 'black-bashing' of the kind we expect from the NT's country Liberal party. The thinking – or lack of it – behind these vicious attacks on Aboriginal religion are too reminiscent of what led to the Kristalnacht in Germany in the 1930s.

We all know what followed. But when do we learn what that meant?

Marcia Langton, 'An Ignorance of Aboriginal Religion', *Sydney Morning Herald*, 23 May 1995

Indigenous voices

The contemporary phase of Indigenous Australian literature began in 1964 with the publication of Oodgeroo Noonuccal's first collection of poetry We Are Going. *This landmark publication became an instant best-seller and, during her lifetime, Oodgeroo was Australia's highest-selling poet by a significant margin. Since the 1960s, Aboriginal and Torres Strait Islander authors have pioneered the publication of works in every state of Australia, in every genre, with a wide variety of themes and concerns. Internationally, works of Aboriginal literature are among the most influential and frequently translated of all Australian writing.*

'People like you don't make the laws.'

Plains of Promise *(1997), Alexis Wright's first novel, tells the story of a young Aboriginal woman called Ivy who is taken from her mother and placed in a mission in South Australia. It speaks of the power of the world of spirits, and of the huge problems facing Indigenous communities: the 'stolen generations', despair and suicide.*

The woman who had killed herself had chosen to move into the small abandoned shed beside Maudie's a week after she arrived at the Mission. She was not eligible for a mission hut – corrugated iron, one-room huts that looked like slight enlargements of outdoor dunnies. They were lined up in rows, with a single tap at the end of every second row. One tap for every two hundred people. They housed what mission authorities referred to as 'nuclear families'. That is, husband and wife with children, no matter how many. If the children had been forcibly removed to the segregated dormitories the couples made room for grandparents, or other extra relatives these people insisted should live with them.

At first Ivy's mother had been placed in the compound of large corrugated iron sheds which housed several families tightly packed together, as well as women alone, with or without children. This was where Ivy had been taken from her. The child was termed a 'half-caste' by the mission bosses and therefore could not be left with the others. Their reasoning: 'It would be a bad influence on these children. We should be able to save them from their kind. If we succeed we will be able to place them in the outside world to make something of themselves. And they will of course then choose to marry white. Thank goodness.

For their children will be whiter and more redeemable in the likeness of God the Father Almighty.'

But Ivy was all the woman had left. The child she gave birth to when she was little more than a child herself. The child of a child and the man who said he loved her during the long, hot nights on the sheep station where she had grown up. She had not seen the likes of a mission before. That was a place where bad Aborigines were sent – as she was frequently warned by the station owners who separated her from her family, to be an older playmate-cum-general help for their own children. So she was always careful she made sure to be good. Even to the man who seduced her by night she was good. She believed in love and he loved her just like her bosses did. With kindness.

At the end of the shearing season she was left to give birth alone, as despised as any other 'general gin' who disgraced herself by confusing lust for kindness and kindness for love.

Years later, when the child Ivy was half-grown, the woman had to be got rid of. In the eyes of her bosses she was not a bad cook for the shearers. 'Now she's had enough practice…since the time we had to put her out of the house to have her bastard child with her own kind.' But the woman was often abusive to everyone. It was said that none of her own people wanted anything to do with her. She was too different, having grown up away from the native compound in the whitefellas' household. And having slept with white men… 'That makes black women like that really uppity,' they said.

'Now she wants to take her kid with her all the time. Even out in the shearers' camp. Won't leave her even with her own family – after all, she is one of

them, isn't she? And the men don't like her either. You know what she went and did? She went and chucked hot fat over one of the fellas when he was just trying to be nice to that child. Cause a right old emergency.' A shrug of the shoulders.

'Yes, might have been the father of the child…who knows. Anyway, she's got to go – this sort of thing only gives the others bad habits…if you don't deal with it properly.'

A magistrate handled the assault matter and handed the finalisation of the woman's affairs over to the Regional Protector of Aborigines, and she was promptly removed. Under ample protection mother and child were delivered into their new world – an Aboriginal world, a world similar to that occupied by thousands of Aboriginal people at the time. In this case, the destination was St Dominic's Mission in the far North.

When Ivy was taken away, her mother had nothing left. The bad Aborigine became morose. A lost number amongst the lost and condemned, 'bad' by the outside world's standards for Blacks. Sentenced to rot for the rest of her days. Even her child taken from her so that the badness of black skin wouldn't rub off.

Her heart stopped dead when they spoke to her just before taking the child, after they had shown her a spot to camp in the squalid stench of the communal shed. It was described as being 'for the good of the child.' Perhaps they were right – but how could she let Ivy go? She felt her whole body had gone numb. Vanished was any sense of the arrogance of the old days now for Number 976-805 on the state's tally books. Her arms and legs felt as though they had been strapped down with weights.

'No, don't,' was all she could think of to say, but the words never passed her lips. Over and over after they left, she thought if only she had said the words out loud, if she had only tried harder, then maybe they would not have taken Ivy away. She had screamed and run after them and tried to drag Ivy away until she was overcome and locked up for a day in the black hole, a place for troublesome blacks. Her release came with a warning of no further interference.

'It is best for you not to be a nuisance. People like you don't make the laws.'

Alexis Wright, *Plains of Promise*, University of Queensland Press, St Lucia, 1997, pp. 11–14

Genetic genocide

In his novel Benang, *Kim Scott evokes the slow progress of the disappearance of Indigenous identity into assimilation and the forgetfulness of an official but fragmented history. Young Harley, who looks white, finds out he is the 'outcome' of several generations of genetic 'blending' carried out by a bureaucracy wanting to whiten the race. His own grandfather is one of the perpetrators of this policy.*

Tap tap. Fingers on the keyboard now. Long after then.

After some time (weeks? months?) of that tap tapping, of house cleaning, of meal preparation, of working in the garden and performing all those necessary domestic chores; after some time of this I found myself drifting along the passage to my grandfather's study. I lacked the confidence to even allow myself to think it, but I wanted evidence of some sort. I wanted confirmation of my fears, what my father and the girls had told me that last time.

The room was neat and well organised. Quite apart from anything else I did it was probably my lack of order, and how I disrupted this, that made the old man rage so in the months to come. Well, as best he could anyway.

I found myself hovering over sets of documents, things filed in plastic envelopes in rumbling drawers and snapping files. Certificates of birth, death, marriage; newspaper clippings, police reports; letters (personal; from this or that historical society); parish records; cemetery listings; books, photographs…

Photographs. As before, I shuffled idly through them. I was careless, letting them fall to the floor. Various people, all classifiable as *Aboriginal*. There were portraits arranged in pairs; one a snapshot labelled *As I found them*, the other a studio photograph captioned *Identical with above child*. There were families grouped according to skin colour. And, sudden enough to startle me, my own image.

A boy. Wing-nut eared and freckled, he wore a school uniform, a tie, a toothy grin. He grinned like an idiot, like an innocent.

Captions to the photographs; *full-blood, half-caste (first cross), quadroon, octoroon*. There was a page of various fractions, possible permutations growing more and more convoluted. Of course, in the language of such mathematics it is simple; from the whole to the partial and back again. This much was clear; I was a fraction of what I might have been.

A caption beneath my father's photograph:

Octoroon grandson (mother quarter-caste [No. 2], father Scottish). Freckles on the face are the only trace of colour apparent.

I saw my image inserted into sequences of three or four in which I was always at the end of the line (even now, I wince at such a phrase). Each sequence was entitled, *Three Generations (Reading from Right to Left)*, and each individual was designated by a fraction.

I was leafing through the papers, letting them fall.

Breeding Up. In the third or fourth generation no sign of native origin is apparent. The repetition of the boarding school process and careful breeding…after two or three generations the advance should be so great that families should be living like the rest of the community.

A cough. Grandad at the door, leaning in its frame.

Such an inadequate memory. What had my father tried to explain?

I turned away from the old man and in a sort of controlled tantrum – oh, no doubt it was childish – I plucked papers from drawers, threw them, let them fall. I made books fly, index cards panic and flee.

Occasionally, rising and falling in all that flurry, I paused to read from a book which had passages underlined on almost every page. There were a couple of family trees inscribed on the flyleaf. Trees? Rather, they were sharply ruled diagrams. My name finished each one. On another page, there was a third, a fourth. All leading to me.

Question marks sprouted in the margins of those diagrams, and I was sowing my own.

Books everywhere, with strips of paper protruding from them like dry and shrivelled tongues.

The need for both biological and social absorption. Dilute the strain.

My grandfather was still in the doorway, now on his knees. One hand clutched his chest, while the other waved feebly at me. I remembered a similar scene, but this time did not flee from him but picked my way among the sprawling books, softly slowly stepped through rustling pages, so sharp-edged and so pale.

Uplift a despised race.

'Well, old man, fuck me white.'
I helped him to his feet.

I would like to say that I remember slowly falling, and how rectangles of white curved and moved aside as if they were sails, and I a great wind. But it was only paper, sheets of paper strewn about me.

And it was there, in a dry and hostile environment, in that litter of paper, cards, files and photographs that I began to settle and make myself substantial. A sterile landscape, but I have grown from that fraction of life which fell.

I understood that much effort had gone into arriving at me. At someone like me. I was intended as the product of a long and considered process which my grandfather had brought to a conclusion.

Ahem.

The whole process – my family history, as it turns out – appealed to Grandad's sense of himself as a scientist who *with his trained mind and keen desire to exert his efforts in the field investigating native culture and in studying the life history of the species, supplies an aid to administration.* He just got lost along the way.

It was the *selective separation from antecedents* which seemed most important, and with which Grandfather was a little lax. It was one of the areas where he had erred with my father.

It was a part of the system used at the settlements and missions.

Kim Scott, *Benang: From the Heart*, Fremantle Arts Centre Press, South Fremantle, 1999, pp. 25–28

'You all make me sick!'

Vivienne Cleven was born in a small town in Western Queensland called Surat in 1968, the region of her Aboriginal homelands. She won the David Unaipon Award for her first novel Bitin' Back *(2001) and she has been acknowledged as one of the most talented contemporary Aboriginal writers.* Bitin' Back *is remarkable for its vibrant use of vernacular Aboriginal English. Cleven's second novel,* Her Sister's Eye, *was first published in 2002. The following extract takes up the story of Murilla, one of the central characters of the book. It takes place on the eve of a special dinner that she is helping to prepare for members of the town's Red Rose Ladies, a committee that Caroline – the wife of the town patriarch – is interested in joining.*

Caroline glanced up from the Asian cookbook. 'What's this?'

'Um, well, since you're so mad on trying to find something that no one else can have, or cook, I thought this might help.' A small smile played at Murilla's mouth. She really didn't think that Caroline would bother.

Caroline, looking puzzled, opened the paper.

Kangaroo Fillet with Orange Sauce
1 x ¼ pound kangaroo fillet
½ cup port
½ cup strawberry jam
½ cup orange juice

⅓ cup red wine vinegar
2 chillies sliced
1 cup beef stock

Cook the Roo Fillets (in an open pan) to medium rare with a small amount of butter and oil and allow to rest. Place the Port, Jam, Orange Juice and Vinegar in a saucepan and simmer slowly until consistency is that of a syrup. Now add the stock to the syrup and simmer until reduced to sauce, then add the Chillies and re-boil prior to serving with the Roo Fillets.

Caroline drew her brows together with a look of absorption. 'Okay, so what does kangaroo taste like?' she queried, looking down at the crumpled paper.

'Let's see…um…It's a tender, red meat, much like rabbit, but sweeter. Good tucker, for sure.' Murilla smiled.

'I doubt any of these Red Rose women would have come across anything like this. It's original and has a certain appeal. And it tastes like rabbit, huh? As crazy as all this sounds, perhaps you're onto something here, Murilla. Being as desperate as I am, I'm willing to try anything once. Okay, when do we start? She folded the paper into a neat square then shoved it into her apron pocket.…

'I say, Caroline, where on earth did you get that brilliant cut of meat!' Polly offered a smile – foxy and fake.

'Oh that! Well now, that's my little secret. I'll tell you this much: you'll never be able to get meat like that in a butcher's shop. Oh no, it's imported. I have a woman in the city that arranges everything for me. It's very, very expensive and few people actually know of it.' Caroline smiled, her fingers drumming on the table.

'That was an extraordinary meal, Caroline, you have really outdone yourself this time!' Gwen exclaimed. 'Now ladies, we really should discuss Caroline's application.'…

'Right then we are. Here Murilla, help me into my coat.' Polly turned around.

Murilla grabbed the coat from the wall hook and then tripped herself forward, right into Polly's back. Hot sauce drenched her and Polly dropped to her knees, squealing and pawing the air with pain and shock. Tamara swung on Murilla, 'You stupid bitch!' she shouted, her face a mottled scarlet as she moved towards Murilla.

Gwen raged, God damn hopeless cow!'

'Useless, useless. Bloody stupid woman! Libby hissed, mouth twisted, eyes gleaming wildly.

Murilla turned. 'Who the hell are you! You all make me sick! Coming here like a bunch of high bitin bitches! I got news for you and that's ya can all go to fucken hell n back!' Murilla made a move at Tamara, her body quivering all over.

A second later Caroline came out into the hall. 'What in God's name!' She looked from Murilla to the women. Realisation etched itself slowly into her features.

Caroline put out a hand. 'Murilla, are you okay?'

'Yeah,' Murilla uttered, nodding at Polly's crumpled form.

'Oh dear, a nasty little accident. Well, hop to your feet, Polly, I'm sure that you'll survive.' Caroline smiled at the group then walked away, a soft laugh trailing her.

'I'll never forget this, Murilla,' Polly spat, as the women gathered around and led her sauce-splattered, indignant figure through the door.

'Neither will I!' Murilla screamed.

There was never to be another dinner party in the Drysdale house.

Vivienne Cleven, *Her Sister's Eye*, University of Queensland Press, St Lucia, 2002, pp. 179–185

BIBLIOGRAPHY

Attwood, Bain, and Andrew Markus, *The Struggle for Aboriginal Rights: A Documentary History*, Allen & Unwin, St Leonards, 1999

Attwood, Bain, *Australie noire, les Aborigènes, un people d'intellectuels*, Autrement Revue, Serie Monde no. 37, Paris, 1989

Bardon, Geoffrey, *Papunya Tula: Art of the Western Desert*, McPhee Gribble, Ringwood, 1991

Barou, Jean-Pierre, *L'œil pense: essai sur les arts primitifs contemporains*, Payot, Paris, 1996

Bell, Diane, *Daughters of the Dreaming*, Spinifex Press, North Melbourne, 2002, 3rd ed.

Benterrak, Krim, Stephen Muecke and Paddy Roe, *Reading the Country: Introduction to Nomadology*, with Ray Keogh, Butcher Joe (Nangan) and E. M. Lohe, Fremantle Arts Centre Press, Fremantle, 1984

Bonnemains, Jacqueline, 'Les artistes du *Voyage de découverte aux Terres Australes* (1800–1804), Charles-Alexandre Lesueur et Nicolas-Martin Petit', in *Bulletin trimestriel de la Société géologique de Normandie et des amis du Muséum du Havre*, 1, Le Havre, 1989

Broome, Richard, *Aboriginal Australians: Black Responses to White Dominance, 1788–2001*, Allen & Unwin, St Leonards, 2002, 3rd ed.

Butor, Michel, *Letters from the Antipodes*, translated *from Boomerang*, introduction and afterword by Michael Spencer, University of Queensland Press, St Lucia, 1981

Campbell, Judy, *Invisible Invaders: Smallpox and Other Diseases in Aboriginal Australia, 1780–1880*, Melbourne University Press, Carlton South, 2002

Caruana, Wally, *Aboriginal Art*, Thames & Hudson, London and New York, 2003, 2nd ed.

Durack, Mary, *Sons in the Saddle*, Constable, London, 1983

Durkheim, Emile, *The Elementary Forms of Religious Life*, trans. Karen E. Fields, Free Press, New York, 1995

Eliade, Mircéa, *Australian Religions: An Introduction*, 'Symbol, Myth and Ritual' series, Cornell University Press, Ithaca, 1973

Elkin, A. P., *The Australian Aborigines*, Angus & Robertson, Sydney, 1974, 5th fully rev. ed.

Freud, Sigmund, *Totem and Taboo: Resemblances between the Psychic Lives of Savages and Neurotics*, trans. A. A. Brill, Routledge, London, 1919

Girardet, Sylvie, Claire Merleau-Ponty and Anne Tardy, *Les Aborigènes d'Australie: grands reportages*, Bayard Editions, Paris, 1991

Glowczewski, Barbara, *Du Rêve à la Loi chez les Aborigènes: mythes, rites et organisation sociale en Australie*, Presses Universitaires de France, Paris, 1991; *Les Rêveurs de désert, people Warlpiri d'Australie*, Actes Sud, Arles, 1996

Haebich, Anna, *For Their Own Good: Aborigines and Government in the South West of Western Australia, 1900–1940*, University of Western Australia Press, Nedlands, 1992, 2nd ed.

Harris, John, *One Blood: 200 Years of Aboriginal Encounter with Christianity: A Story of Hope*, Albatross Books, Sutherland, 1994, 2nd ed.

Horton, David (gen. ed.), *The Encyclopædia of Aboriginal Australia: Aboriginal and Torres Strait Islander History, Society and Culture*, Aboriginal Studies Press for the Australian Institute of Aboriginal and Torres Strait Islander Studies, Canberra, 1994, 2 vols.

Isaacs, Jennifer (ed.), *Australian Dreaming: 40,000 Years of Aboriginal History*, Ure Smith, Sydney, 1992

Kleinert, Sylvia, and Margot Neale (eds), *The Oxford Companion to Aboriginal Art and Culture*, Oxford University Press, Melbourne, 2000

Kupka, Karel, *Dawn of Art: Painting and Sculpture of Australian Aborigines*, foreword by A. P. Elkin, Angus & Robertson, Sydney, 1965; *Peintres aborigènes d'Australie*, Musée de l'Homme, Paris, 1972

Lévi-Strauss, Claude, *The Savage Mind*, Weidenfeld and Nicolson, London, 1972

Lonely Planet: Aboriginal Australia & the Torres Strait Islands – guide to Indigenous Australia, Lonely Planet Publications, Melbourne, 2001

Morgan, Sally, *My Place*, Virago, London, 1988

Mudrooroo, *Long Live Sandawara*, Hyland House, Melbourne, 1987; *Master of the Ghost Dreaming*, Angus & Robertson, Sydney, 1991

Mulvaney, John, and Johan Kamminga, *The Prehistory of Australia*, Allen & Unwin, St Leonards, 1999

Mundine, Djon, 'L'art aborigène de l'Australie contemporaine', in *Les Cahiers du musée national d'Art moderne*, Paris, summer 1989

National Museum of Victoria, *The Aboriginal Photographs of Baldwin Spencer*, introduced by John Mulvaney, selected and annotated by Geoffrey Walker, Viking O'Neil in association with the National Museum of Victoria Council, Ringwood, 1987

Pedersen, Howard, *Jandamarra and the Bunuba Resistance*, Magabala Books, Broome, 2000

Perkins, Hetty, and Hannah Fink (eds), *Papunya Tula: Genesis and Genius*, Art Gallery of New South Wales, Sydney, 2000

Reynolds, Henry, *Black Pioneers*, Penguin, Ringwood and Harmondsworth, 2000

Rose, Deborah Bird, *Dingo Makes us Human: Life and Land in an Aboriginal Australian Culture*, Cambridge University Press, Oakleigh, 2000, 2nd ed.

Rose, Michael (ed.), *For the Record: 160 years of Aboriginal Print Journalism*, Allen & Unwin, St Leonards, 1996

Scott, Kim, *Benang: From the Heart*, Fremantle Arts Centre Press, Fremantle, 1999

Shoemaker, Adam, *Black Words, White Page: Aboriginal Literature, 1929–1988*, University of Queensland Press, St Lucia, 1992, 2nd ed.

Spencer, Baldwin and F. J. Gillen, *The Native Tribes of Central Australia*, Dover Publications, New York, 1968

Stanner, W. E. H., 'Religion, Totemism and Symbolism', in R. M. Berndt and C. H. Berndt, *Aboriginal Man in Australia*, Angus & Robertson, Sydney, 1965

Strehlow, T. G. H., *Aranda Traditions*, Angus & Robertson, Sydney, 1947

Swain, Tony, *A Place for Strangers: Towards a History of Australian Aboriginal Being*, Cambridge University Press, Cambridge, 1993

Tench, Watkin, *Sydney's First Four Years: Being a Reprint of A Narrative of the Expedition to Botany Bay and A Complete Account of the Settlement at Port Jackson*, introduction and annotations by L. F. Fitzhardinge, Angus & Robertson, Sydney, 1961

Turbet, Peter, *The Aborigines of the Sydney District Before 1788*, Kangaroo Press, East Roseville, 2001, rev. ed.

Tweedie, Penny, *Indigenous Australia Standing Strong*, Simon & Schuster, East Roseville, 2001

Wright, Alexis, *Plains of Promise*, University of Queensland Press, St Lucia, 1997

Exhibition Catalogues

Barou, Jean-Pierre and Sylvie Crossman (eds), *Peintres aborigènes d'Australie, le Rêve de la fourmi à miel*, Grande Halle de la Villette, Paris, 1997

Caruana, Wally (ed.), *Likan'Mirri – Connections: The AIATSIS Collection of Art*, Australian National University, Canberra, 2004

Isaacs, Jennifer, *Aboriginality: Contemporary Aboriginal Paintings & Prints*, University of Queensland Press, St Lucia, 1992

Ryan, Judith, *Ginger Riley*, National Gallery of Victoria, Melbourne, 1997

B elow, a Bora ceremony, *c.* 1900–27.

LIST OF ILLUSTRATIONS

INDEX

PHOTO CREDITS

AFP 60, 84–85, 92–93. AFP/Pictor, 81. AFP/Torsten Blackwood 70. AKG, Paris/Werner Forman 33. Allport Library and Museum of Fine Arts, State Library of Tasmania 18b. The Art Archive 28, 29. The Art Archive/British Library 12a. The Art Archive/Royal Commonwealth Society/E. Tweedy 24–25. Art Resource/J. Steele 38l. Australian Picture Library 67, 68b. Australian War Memorial, Canberra 73. Battye Library, Perth/Susan Stretch 62–63. Bridgeman-Giraudon 14–15, 15r, 24a, 26, 27, 56. Corbis/Yann Arthus-Bertrand 40–41. Corbis/Bettman 34, 78–79. Corbis/E. Hoppe 68–69. Corbis/Dave G. Houser 20. Corbis/Hulton 65a. Corbis/Alan Towse/Ecoscene 47. Corbis/Penny Tweedie 1, 2–3, 6–7, 21, 34–35a, 42–43, 44, 52–53, 76, 83. DR 75, 86, 88–89, 90, 91, 110. Getty Images/Hulton 57. Getty Images/Penny Tweedie 4–5. Getty Images/Taxi 55. Magnum/Thomas Hoepker 22a. Musée de l'Homme, Paris 11, 22b, 30, 46, 48b, 50, 51, 54, 97, 99, 101. Musée de l'Homme, Paris/J.-C. Mazur 35r. Muséum d'Histoire naturelle, Le Havre 10, 12b, 13, 17a, 17c, 17b, 18a, 19. National Gallery of Australia, Canberra 31, 51l, 71, 77, 82, 87. National Gallery of Victoria 96. National Library of Australia, Canberra 59b, 61, 64–65. RMN 9. RMN/J.-G. Berrizi spine, 38r, 41c. RMN/J. Blot 45l. RMN/D. Arnaudet 45r. RMN/H. Lewandowski, 39. Rue des Archives/Varma 59a. Sipa/DPPI 85b. Sipa Press/AP 48a. State Library of New South Wales 14b, 32, 36a, 36b, 37a, 37b, 42b, 72, 74, 121. Sydney Morning Herald 105. Penny Tweedie, Hawkhurst 80–81, 94l, 94r, 95l, 95r. © ADAGP, Paris 2002 51l, 87.

ACKNOWLEDGMENTS

The authors would like to thank Bain Attwood, Ann Curthoys, Rosamund Dalziell, Celine Faivre, Peter Hiscock, Shireen Huda, Ian Keen, Campbell Macknight, Francesca Merlan and Howard Morphy for their valuable advice, and in particular Françoise Plassais, who had the original idea for this book. Thanks also to Jean-Pierre Barou, Sylvie Crossmann and Laurent Dousset for their helpfulness and skill, and to the staff at Thames & Hudson.

Stephen Muecke is Professor of Cultural Studies at the University of Technology, Sydney, and is a Fellow of the Australian Academy of the Humanities. His books include(with Paddy Roe and Krim Benterrak): *Reading the Country: Introduction to Nomadology* (1996) and *No Road (bitumen all the way)* (1997). His *Ancient & Modern: Time, Culture and Indigenous Philosophy* will appear in 2004.

Adam Shoemaker is Professor and Dean of the Faculty of Arts at the Australian National University in Canberra. He has also been a visiting professor at the University of Toulouse-le-Mirail and at the University of Antwerp. He has written or edited seven books dealing with Australian Indigenous cultures, literatures and race relations, including *Black Words, White Page* (1989); *Oodgeroo: A Tribute* (1994) and David Unaipon's *Legendary Tales of the Australian Aborigines* (2001: co-edited by Stephen Muecke).

Every effort has been made to trace the copyright holders of the texts contained in the Documents section of this book, and we apologize in advance for any unintentional omissions. We would be pleased to insert the appropriate acknowledgment in any subsequent edition of this publication.

First published in the United Kingdom in 2004 by Thames & Hudson Ltd, 181A High Holborn, London WC1V 7QX

www.thamesandhudson.com

British Library Cataloguing-in-Publication Data

A catalogue record for this book is available from the British Library

ISBN 0-500-30114-X

Printed and bound in Italy